# THE COMPLETELY UNAUTHORIZED
# HOWARD STERN

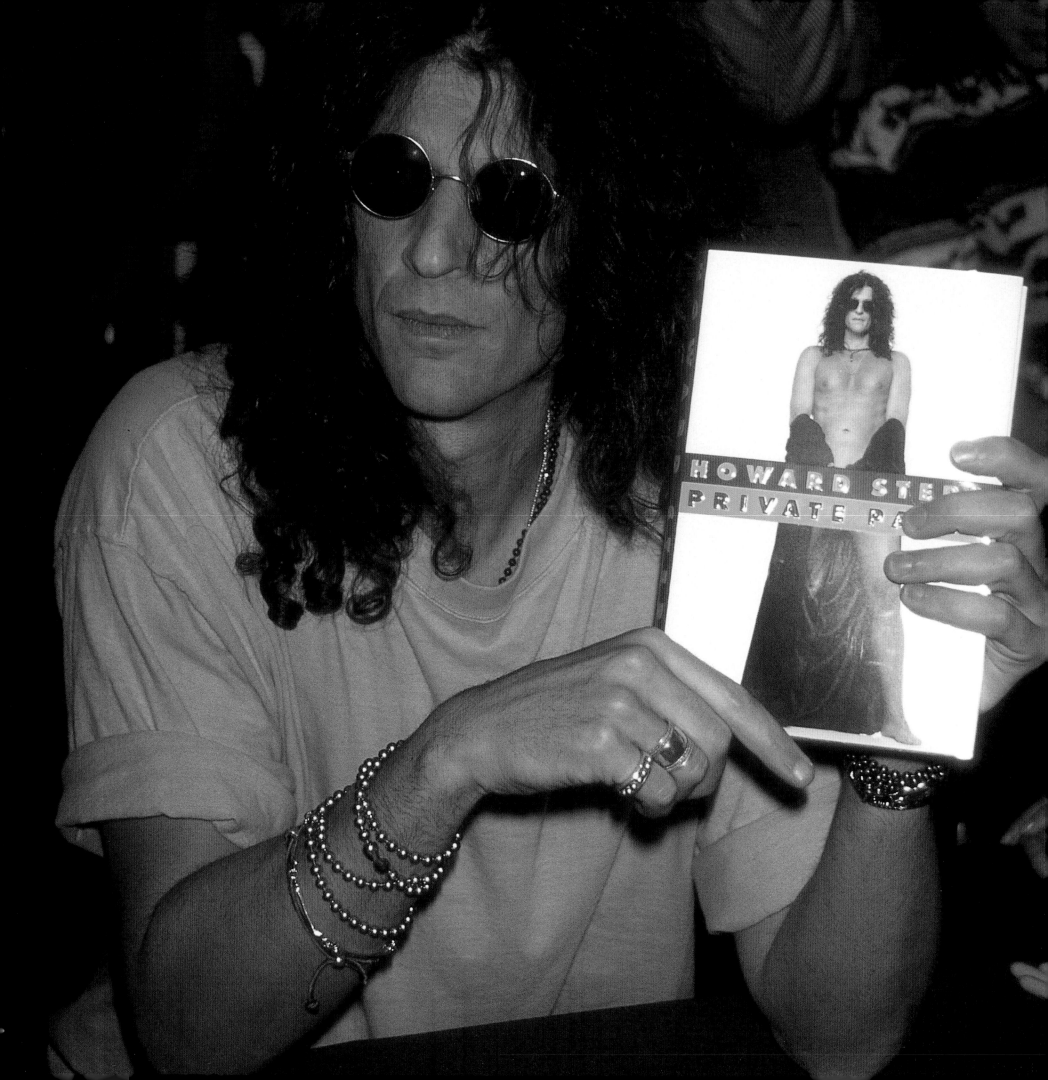

# THE COMPLETELY UNAUTHORIZED HOWARD STERN

## BY MATTHEW HOFFMAN

COURAGE BOOKS

AN IMPRINT OF RUNNING PRESS
PHILADELPHIA • LONDON

1   3   5   7   9   10   8   6   4   2   1

Digit on the right indicates the number of this printing.

Library of Congress Cataloging-in-Publication Number 97-77968

ISBN 0-7624-0377-2

**Front cover photograph: Retna Limited U.S.A./©Scott Weiner**
**Back cover photograph: Everett Collection**

Editor: Francine Hornberger
Photography Editor: Valerie E. Kennedy

Printed in Hong Kong
Color separations by Hong Kong Scanner Arts Int'l Ltd.

This book may be ordered by mail from the publisher.
***But try your bookstore first!***

Published by Courage Books, an imprint of
Running Press Book Publishers
125 South Twenty-second Street
Philadelphia, Pennsylvania 19103-4399

# ACKNOWLEDGMENTS

Special thanks to the following individuals and organizations:
Charles & Elisha Abrams, Evan Alboum, Gabrielle Allabashi, Todd Andrews, Irving & Lori Belateche and family, Peter Bernard, Robin Brownstein, Deborah, Joe Dunn, Todd and Doreen Eliassen, Jim Eshom, John Falchi, Tony Felicetta, Woody Fincher, Rickie Freundlich, Alan & Ella Friedman and family, Peter Guttmacher, Henry, J. David & Lora Hoffman, Barbara, David, Drew & Robert Hoffman, Francine Hornberger, Janette Jensen, Jason, Ted & Sally Jensen, Valerie E. Kennedy, Mark E. Lang, Rick Louis, Kevin Lowenthal, Robin & Gina McAuley, Adam Menken, Dori Mock, Marie Mundaca, Deidre Myles, Andrew Nelson, Bill Norrett, Jason Norrett, Ryan Rickets, Marilyn Saunders, Ali Sherwin, Phil Silver, Stephen Slaybaugh, Bob Stein, Rachael, Tess & Wesley Wei, James Wilson and family, Michael Winnick, Gerald Zeigerman, Lee Zimmerman, Alison & Igor Zomb, The Beverly Hills Library, The Margaret Herrick Library, The Museum of Television and Radio.

# CONTENTS

"I think most guys are like me. . . . I believe that I might be EVERY guy."

# CHAPTER ONE

# Portrait of the Anarchist as a Young Man

In the mid-1950s, two events took place that would forever alter the face of broadcast entertainment. At radio station WOR in New York, an engineer devised the seven-second delay for talk radio pioneer Long John Nebel. This development not only paved the way for interactive radio but ensured its future. Nearby, in Jackson Heights, Queens, a son was born to radio engineer Ben Stern and his wife, Ray, on January 12, 1954. Howard Stern would grow up to be one of the greatest forces in this medium, defining and defiling the not-so-venerable outlet known as talk radio. Additionally, Stern would enjoy massive success pursuing ventures in other realms of the pop culture environment, thus earning the sobriquet of self-proclaimed "King of All Media."

In 1955, the upwardly mobile Stern family (Ben, Ray, Howard, and older sister, Ellen) moved outward, east of the five boroughs, to Roosevelt, a Long Island suburb. Roosevelt was a growing Nassau County community that, in the early 1950s, was remarkably integrated considering Long Island's primarily white demographic. For young Howard the effects of this move would be far-reaching. While Roosevelt suffered serious functional problems as a racially mixed community, the Stern household also revealed its own form of dysfunction at this time. Developmentally, these could be designated Howard's *de*formative years. In his book *Private Parts*, Stern describes his mother as being extremely overprotective and declares that she raised him "like a veal. It was like growing up in a box with no lights on." According to Stern, his overly attentive mother not only filled him with guilt and fear ("To this day, I can't go out of the house for more than five minutes without worrying that something bad is going to happen to me") but humiliated him by monitoring his temperature rectally until his eighteenth year. Stern's relationship with his father was embarrassing for other reasons. Stern claims that he received the brunt of his father's frequent tirades ("I was the designated yellee"), which could come without warning from out of nowhere.

Stern's first forays into show business were fairly benign. At the age of seven, young Howard entertained the denizens of a local old-age home with marionette shows in a portable puppet theater built by his father. The youthful puppeteer supplied a soundtrack to his extravaganzas using a recording of the Broadway production of *Fiddler on the Roof*. In *Private Parts*, Stern remembers, "At the end of the night, I was handed an envelope with ten bucks inside! What a windfall! Getting paid good money for something you enjoyed was definitely a trip."

Stern has remarked that his mother is responsible for his initial creative expression. Ray Stern believed that she could encourage sensitivity and foster creativity in her male child by introducing dolls into Howard's playtime. She settled on marionettes so as to save her son from the childhood trauma of being assailed by his peers for such an unmanly practice. Unwittingly, Ray provided her son with an outlet for an outrageously comical expression of prepubescent sexuality.

Not content with entertaining the highly appreciative yet somewhat clueless geriatrics, Howard the entertainer treated his friends to puerile pornographic puppetry in his basement. By Stern's

**Previous page (Inset):** Stern's 1972 high school yearbook picture. **Opposite:** At a book signing, Stern has a firm hold on his *Private Parts* as his wife and parents look on.

# The Origins of Talk Radio

Howard Stern's accomplishments in the genre of talk radio are all the more remarkable when one considers the history of the medium. In the early 1950s, New York talk radio pioneer Barry Gray reportedly became the first radio personality to broadcast an on-air telephone conversation. When bandleader-musician Woody Herman telephoned Gray during his broadcast, Gray took the call on the air. He immediately fielded a follow-up call from a listener who wondered if it was really Woody Herman at the other end of the line. Thus, according to Gray, "The talk show was born."

An adoptive father of this newborn radio format was Long John Nebel. Nebel, a former street vendor in New York, went on to open his own auction house, where he caught the ears of executives for the Mutual Radio Network. In 1956, the inveterate huckster Nebel hit the airwaves and took Gray's advance one step further. Nebel's contentious, often disagreeable style ("I don't give a damn whether you believe it or not") and consummate skills as a salesman prefigured many of today's talk radio personalities.

The outspoken Nebel claims to have originated the idea of two-way conversation on radio. An engineer at radio station WOR developed the technology of the seven-second delay. This electronic cushion between when something was said and the time it was broadcast allowed callers to go on-air "live." This was groundbreaking—talk radio would never be the same again. The next massive upheaval would come more than two decades later, when Howard Stern would enter the scene and, with seismic intensity, forever alter the talk radio soundscape.

accounts, these displays involved freeform orgiastic marionette combinations. With the addition of a horse puppet, bestiality was thrown in for bad measure. Of course, Stern's boyhood pals were delighted by the demonstration to which the perverse puppeteer added his own off-color commentary. Stern also employed a Jerry Mahoney doll and offered "X-rated" ventriloquism to his pals. Although Stern recounts these "dirty puppet shows" with amusement in *Private Parts*, he adds an unusually wistful, nostalgic note as a coda: "I had ruined a beautiful innocent part of my life." Given his reputation as a spokesman for the testosterone-rich male id, it is rare to catch Stern reminiscing longingly for his lost innocence.

# Puppetry, Perversion, and Power

When the young Howard Stern used his marionettes to express his precociously ribald sense of humor, little did he know that he was continuing in the grand tradition of world theater.

According to Grolier's encyclopedia, "The Greco-Turkish Karaghiozis shadow play [a form of puppet theater]...offered robust, often obscenely satirical fare to village audiences." What better description could be applied to Stern's puppet performances for his childhood chums?

Grolier's goes on to say that "under fascist regimes, puppets [permit] a freedom of satirical comment prohibited in other media." This reference neatly parallels Stern's description of his beloved mother having run "her household with the intensity of Hitler" and the suggestion that he was raised "like a veal."

Curiously, Stern still enjoys and encourages playing with dolls. On his syndicated radio show, more than one member of Stern's radio family has had his way with RealDoll—an anatomically correct, highly realistic sex doll.

# What's the Matter? Are You Stupid?

When Howard was in grammar school, Ben Stern co-owned Aura Recording, Inc., a sound studio in midtown Manhattan. Howard would occasionally visit the studio with his father. Here, Howard was exposed to professional animation voiceover artists such as Don Adams (Tennessee Tuxedo) and Wally Cox (Underdog). Popular artists of the day and well-known show business celebrities engaged in their craft and left an indelible impression on the young Howard.

In an interview with Robert Wilonsky for *New Times*, Stern recollected, "I used to watch them do these sketches, this cartoon shtick, and I thought this was exciting." These early encounters were revelatory in their impact for Stern, as

*"When I hear myself on the radio sometimes and I'm really, you know, ripping into somebody, I know it's my father. My father ripped into me on a daily basis. . . . I hear my father coming out of me and it just goes off, you know, and it's very much how my father dealt with me. "*

he remarked to Marshall Fine in *Playboy*: "Even at an early age, I remember wanting to be on radio, wanting to do a show as opposed to sitting there and playing records. My father bought me a tape recorder and I would sit in my room and do radio shows—but not like what I heard on the radio. I would do hours of sketches and voices and all kinds of shit. I wanted to have fun and entertain people."

Howard's inspiration to do something different in radio came to him while accompanying his father during his commute to work. It occurred to the perceptive youth that the stale formats of radio offered limited entertainment value and provided precious little diversion from the nerve-jangling, mind-numbing travails of rush-hour traffic. In fact,

the only moments that seized the youngster's attention were when things would go wrong in the studio—instances where somebody goofed or dropped something in the background. The lad was firmly convinced that, were he ever to have a radio show, he would pull back the veil for all to see what goes on. True to his childhood vision, Stern today offers the public a warts-and-all radio experience.

Stern's nascent explorations in broadcasting served to lay the groundwork for his revolutionary approach to the medium known as talk radio. On a Wollensack tape recorder, a gift from his father, nine-year-old Howard was already experimenting with format and developing what would become his unique approach to radio. However, it is not Howard's recordings of this era that have become legendary in the Stern media empire. Rather, the irascible Ben Stern is responsible for one of the most hysterically funny and constantly revisited bits of Stern lore.

On an annual basis, Howard, his older sister, Ellen, and their cousins would make a pilgrimage to the Aura Recording studios where Ben Stern would capture the playful children on audiotape. Throughout the years, Howard has frequently referred to his father's volatile disposition in the early days and has declared that Ben Stern's "favorite sport was yelling." When a tape of one such session surfaced years later, Stern hit payback dirt. Here was a recording that made it abundantly clear that Stern's unfavorable representations of his father's rants were no exaggeration. Armed with proof, Stern aired the recordings on his radio show. Thus began a legacy.

Ben Stern's interview of the grammar-school-age Howard begins ominously enough:

**BEN:** Howard, I don't want any foolish answers from you, otherwise don't answer.

The elder Stern continues:

**BEN:** Don't scream and don't talk....not too close. When I give you the signal.

**HOWARD:** What should I say?

**BEN:** What's the matter, are you stupid?

Having filled his subject with dread in the tradition of the grand inquisitor Torquemada, Ben Stern interrogated his son so as to elicit Howard's opinion of international affairs pertaining the United States' involvement with the United Nations; Howard was about seven years old at the time! Displeased with Howard's xenophobic response involving mimetic machine gun sounds following the remark "'Cause we don't want the Japs anymore," Ben Stern verbally struck back with the phrase now infamous to legions of Stern listeners:

**BEN:** I told you not to be stupid, you moron!

Reworking this evidence of his early emotional trauma into comedy, Stern crafted a hilarious mock advertisement for the Ben Stern Day Care Center. Promises such as "Any spark of vitality will be eradicated by our professionals" are intercut with the motto "Shut up, sit down!"—an oft-repeated classic Stern sound bite. To Ben Stern's defense comes no greater apologist than Howard himself. In an interview with Maer Roshan for *New York Magazine*, Stern confessed that his father's verbal assaults helped to form his radio personality: "He had a great way of cutting me off when I got boring, when I got too dull.... He could be cruel, but he was also very supportive.... My parents were very loving, but at the same time, you know, nobody's perfect."

## It Takes a Village to Raze a Child

Apart from his father's verbal abuse, Howard suffered at the hands (and the fists) of the residents of his progressively *dis*-integrated Roosevelt community. By the time Howard had reached the seventh grade, white homeowners began to move out of Roosevelt in droves, leaving middle-class blacks as the majority citizenship. Howard attended Roosevelt Junior-Senior High School, where he claims there were only a handful of whites, but his yearbook from this epoch reveals that roughly one-third of Stern's classmates were Caucasian.

Stern's memories may not jibe entirely with an actual census or demographic analysis of Roosevelt circa 1968-1969, but one major truth surfaces—life in Roosevelt

was tough on the long-suffering and long-legged awkward teenager. He wasn't the proverbial outsider looking in; he was looking to get away.

Stern has drawn upon his tainted well of memories regarding Roosevelt throughout his radio years. As with many of his unpleasant experiences, Stern has used this one to comic effect while making some rather trenchant social observations about race relations and hypocrisy in the liberal agenda of integration. In an interview for the television news magazine *20/20*, Stern recalled:

"I grew up in an all-black neighborhood. Everyone was talking to each other about race. That's all we talked about. In classes...the teachers were all phonies, they couldn't even handle the discussion. They would talk about how we should all live together as brothers and we should all be together. What a bunch of hooey. They're sitting in an all-black neighborhood, I'm the only white guy living there, talking about how we should all live together as brothers? Meanwhile, they're not even living in the town where I go to school, these teachers."

Ben and Ray Stern proudly display their son Howard's magnum opus.

*"Whenever we would tune in and hear anything remotely interesting, even if a guy dropped a tape in the background, you know, I would go, wow, what was that? That was interesting. If I had a radio show, I would put that on the air and explain what was going on."*

Stern at K-Rock in 1986—the beginning
of his longest-running radio gig.

In retrospect, Stern commends his parents for their bravery in not initially joining the widespread white exodus. At the time, however, the gangly teenager was a miserable outcast who was regularly beaten up for lunch money and robbed of personal property ("They'd take your fucking pants!"). All efforts toward assimilation were met with failure, and Stern found it impossible to ingratiate himself with his schoolmates. Among his peers, racial tensions escalated with diminishing tolerance for the dwindling white population.

Stern recalls that the intelligent black students were transported by bus to an upscale learning institution. He characterizes the remaining students at Roosevelt as "mutants," making the young scholar "one of the brightest kids in the school." Being at the top of a heap of what he refers to as mentally defective high schoolers offered Stern little consolation.

Despite their son's relentless pleading to flee Roosevelt, Ben and Ray Stern's eventual decision to join the white diaspora was the result of one unfortunate event. When one of Howard's black friends was viciously attacked "for hanging out with a honky," the Sterns realized that, sadly, the integration experiment had failed horribly. These experiences had a profound and permanent effect on Stern's psyche, as indicated by his remarks to David Remnick in *The New Yorker*: "If there's any reason I have sort of a skeptical view of the world, it's Roosevelt.... I guess that left me a little demoralized and down on humanity."

## Uncivil Rites

In 1969, the Stern clan packed up and moved approximately two miles (3.2km) west to Rockville Centre, a predominantly white, affluent community. Incorporated in 1893, Rockville Centre had the feel of a New England village. At first glance the new environs appeared to be an improvement. Scratching the surface, the fifteen-year-old Stern soon discovered an entirely new level of hypocrisy.

At South Side Senior High School, a practically all-white institution (blacks represented less than 5 percent of the student body), Stern encountered more high-minded philosophizing about brotherhood. It was clear that these polemicists were precisely the type of "phonies" who would pack up the moment too many dark faces moved into their lily-white community. In Roosevelt, Howard experienced "being white as a negative thing." In Rockville Centre, he discovered he wasn't white enough. An ironic twist of fate placed the Stern's new domicile near a golf course that barred Jews from playing. So much for learning to live together. The "freaked-out" adolescent felt condemned to being a perpetual outsider with nowhere to run. Stern withdrew into himself.

## Two Half and Half Not

In high school in Rockville Centre, Stern sensed an insidious undercurrent of anti-Semitism from a large contingent of the students. Curiously, Stern has referred to himself as half-Jewish, half-Italian, half-black, or half-Cherokee depending on the context and to whom he is speaking. Yet both of his parents are of Austro-Hungarian Jewish descent. Most listeners realize that Stern's declarations often rely on exaggeration and even prevarication. For those who aren't in on the joke...that's where the fun begins.

Throughout the years, Stern has incited and amused listeners with such bits as "Hill Street Jews," a spoof on the police drama Hill Street Blues in which the detectives speak in heavy Yiddish accents. Another feature is the long-running call-in segment "Guess Who's the Jew," featuring cohort Fred Norris assuming the identity of arch-Nazi Kurt Waldheim, Jr. In this segment, Stern regularly exposes "contestants" as harboring anti-Semitic opinions. Another favorite target is Kathie Lee Gifford (who is, in fact, half-Jewish), whom Stern derides as Kathie "Jew" Gifford, presumably due to her ardent Christianity, which he views as sanctimonious.

As for Stern's "half-Jew" status, by claiming mixed affiliation, Stern is afforded the liberty of making jokes at the expense of Jews and non-Jews. Stern uses the fact that he was raised in an "all-black" neighborhood as his license to indulge in ethnic and racial humor that most other white performers tend to avoid. Stern is, indeed, an equal-opportunity offender.

Still playing with dolls, Stern holds a diapered puppet version of himself.

By most accounts of his high school classmates and teachers, as related to Stern biographer Paul D. Colford, the future radio star's teenage persona was unremarkable. Evidently Stern exhibited an awkward shyness, an effect of introversion that belied a subtle, anarchic sense of humor. In an interview with the Arts & Entertainment Network, Stern's classmate and friend Scott Passeser recalled:

> "Howard was devoid of the major things that people approve of in high school...athletic ability, scholastic ability, abilities with females.... On top of that, he was nicknamed..."Gunky" because he was so incredibly awkward. He couldn't run, he couldn't jump, he had no physical prowess whatsoever in any sport and he stayed away from it. He hardly went to gym. He cut gym as often as he could. And he became...such a standout, that we were sort of attracted to him because we wanted to know how could a guy be so, so, so different. How could a guy be six-foot-five, fourteen years old, and not be able to play basketball?"

Passeser's unflattering portrait of his high school friend confirms Stern's assertion that he grew up a perennial outcast. Interestingly, Passeser touches on a memory that indicates one direction in which Stern's humor would move. While playing poker with a handful of friends, Stern would "take a big gulp of soda and just have a giant belch and we would laugh, like idiots, we laughed at him. So the more we laughed at his raunchiness, the more raunchiness he wanted to give us."

The origins of Stern's comedy are firmly rooted in what the academic may call borborygmus and crepitus—the layman knows these as burping and farting. Stern admits,

The woman whom Stern acknowledges loved him before he had a radio show, his wife, Alison.

"He always knew he'd be real big. . . . Howard was always made to feel that he was special. He doesn't need to be the life of the party, but he needs to be famous. When he's not performing, he's rarely on—he's a real stick-in-the-mud."

—Alison Stern, Howard's wife

"Burping is still so funny to me. Maybe I'm caught in, you know, terminal adolescence, but a guy sitting and belching a really loud belch will break me up. And farting is one of the most wonderful things. The noise itself is a symphony to me." According to one of Stern's high school teachers, Richard Caproni, "As far as I was concerned, he just kinda passed through." Perhaps he was just passing gas.

Eager to escape the "prison" of high school, Stern missed his graduation ceremony in 1972, to arrive on time for the summer session at Camp Wel-Met, where he worked as a dishwasher. A sleep-away camp located in the Catskill Mountains, Wel-Met derived its name from the Metropolitan Jewish Welfare Board with which it was affiliated. As a camper, Stern met his first girlfriend, and throughout the summers he found opportunities to pursue a number of sexual liaisons. (Stern offers an explicitly detailed account of these and later sexual adventures in *Private Parts*.)

In the relaxed camp atmosphere the awkward teen was less constrained. Nonetheless, Stern maintained a reticent demeanor and gave little indication of his future career objectives. A fellow camper recalls but one instance when Stern overcame his taciturnity and revealed his ambition to become a radio star of the highest magnitude.

In *Howard Stern A-Z*, Luigi Lucaire significantly notes that while Stern has attended at least one camp reunion, he has been conspicuously absent from any high school reunion.

## It Had to B.U.

In the fall of 1972, Stern was matriculated at Boston University. Although he was in the top of his class at Roosevelt, Stern graduated from South Side in Rockville Centre an average student with fair SAT scores. Because of his scholastic underachievements, Stern was required to enter Boston University through its College of Basic Studies, a two-year proving ground in which students of unremarkable intellect had to demonstrate their academic mettle before entering the university proper. Reportedly, Stern referred to the College of Basic Studies (renamed the College of General Studies) as "the dumb shit school."

To Stern, Boston University was attractive for two reasons: it was known as a party school ("I heard it was an excellent place to pick up women"), and more crucially, it offered an

ingress into the radio business. WBUR-FM, heard widely throughout Boston, was located in the University's School of Public Communications. But it was not until his sophomore year that Stern finally got a chance to explore his chosen field on the anemic campus radio station WBTU-AM. WBTU's signal barely had the strength to reach the university buildings, but radio it was. Stern was provided an air shift and proceeded to suffer an embarrassingly disastrous radio debut. The inexperienced disc jockey managed to knock a cart rack over onto a spinning Santana record during his inauspicious maiden voyage onto the airwaves. Frazzled, yet undeterred, Stern hung in and performed a variety of broadcast tasks for the station. But his sights were set on comedy.

The novice broadcaster teamed up with three upperclassmen and set out to provide more amplitude than modulation to the station's format. The comedic construct was *The King Schmaltz Bagel Hour* (a send-up of the syndicated *The King Biscuit Flour Hour*). Considered outrageous for 1973, this comic radio venture was grounded during its first flight. Immediately following the segment "Godzilla Goes to Harlem," in which the fire-breathing legend of Japanese monster filmdom is almost mistaken for an Italian and mugged in Harlem, Stern and the gang were fired. Summarily dismissed, radio's future "bad boy" was anything but discouraged. Stern maintained a belief in the validity of his specific approach to radio and was determined to pursue the direction indicated by his personal creative compass.

As his sophomore year came to an end, Stern found himself cramming to complete a final project, a group term paper that was to investigate notions of utopian societies. Stern and his classmates were supposed to have worked on it throughout the semester but left it until the eleventh hour. Stern, Ellen Fruchtman, Kevin Goldman, and two other students worked throughout a weekend of all-nighters in a cramped hotel room. According to Fruchtman, Stern's chief efforts during this writing session involved trying to get one of the girls into bed with him. Stern's sexual advances thwarted, he ended up having to share a bed with Goldman, who notes that Stern wore a hairnet to bed: "How can you not love a guy who wears a hairnet?" Despite his amorous failure, Stern and his fellow students succeeded in producing a paper that was rewarded with a passing grade.

Costumed and made up to re-create his regrettable late 1970s look, Stern takes a break during the filming of *Private Parts*.

In a scene from *Private Parts*, Stern relives the early days of his relationship with Alison, portrayed here by actress Mary McCormack.

Stern matriculated into the School of Public Communications in the general population of Boston University in his junior year. A chance encounter with his future wife, Alison Berns, a social work major from Newton, Massachusetts, has been described by Stern as "the most incredible highlight of my miserable life." Stern regarded his sexual adventures up until this point as nightmarish. Things would be different with Alison.

Stern's first efforts to pursue a serious relationship involved persuading a reluctant Alison to star in a film project he was required to do for one of his classes. The eight-millimeter film documentary on transcendental meditation (TM), initially devised as a tool of seduction, was ultimately voted best film of the year by Stern's professors. (In fact, to this day, Stern practices TM before and after his radio broadcasts to clear his mind and energize his spirit.) As with his certainty regarding radio, Stern was convinced that Alison was the girl for him. In *Private Parts*, Stern relates, "I was so punch drunk from getting knocked around by women that I couldn't imagine someone this dynamite would be into me."

On their first date, Howard and Alison went to see the film *Lenny*, based on the life of Lenny Bruce, which Stern remarked "was a pretty good indication of our life to come." Following the movie, the couple went to Howard's abode, where he plied his date with a bottle of Blue Nun and made it to third base. Hoping to make it to home plate, Howard learned that Alison would not have sex on the first date. Despite his imprecations as to the absurdity of her injunction against conjunction, Alison prevailed and Howard was forced to wait until their second date to "close the deal." Stern had reached a new level of emotional and sexual maturity. He recalled, "I was totally into Alison. Within a week after our relationship began I knew I was going to marry her." Stern, who had never before had a meaningful sexual relationship, was already picturing growing old with his new-found love.

In 1976, Stern graduated from Boston University magna cum laude. Almost immediately, he was hired by WNTN-AM, a progressive rock station located in Newton, Massachusetts. The up-and-coming disc jockey was thrilled—this sort of instant success was not to be believed. Sadly, the situation revealed itself to be less than ideal when the newest member of the WNTN team discovered on payday there was no remuneration for his on-air efforts. Although eager to work in his chosen medium, Stern had no desire to work for free. Notwithstanding the brevity of his first professional radio gig, Stern came out of the experience with a tape worthy of presenting to prospective employers.

Stern moved back to Rockville Centre to be near Alison (who was attending Columbia University at the time, working toward a master's degree in social work) and to seek work in the New York radio market. Since childhood, Stern had dreamed of hitting it big in the Big Apple's radio scene. Stern recalls looking down on New York City while flying home during his college years and thinking, "One day, every one of these homes will be hearing me on their radio." To his friends and family these aspirations seemed like pipe dreams, but Stern would demonstrate, much to everyone's surprise but his own, that New York was just the beginning. As he would soon realize, however, the highway to fame and fortune would be pitted with potholes, covered with obstacles, and policed by idiot law enforcement officers.

W-4, Stern's Detroit radio home, changed its programming to Country virtually overnight. Stern reenacts the beginning of his end at the Motor City station in *Private Parts*.

"I guess it's true that I'm down on humanity. Every-body is such a phony and a two-face. Everyone pretty much accepts that everybody else is lying. The world is not a very pretty place."

# CHAPTER TWO

# The Misshapen Things to Come

Shortly after returning to Rockville Centre, Stern was approached with a job offer by Donald Jay Barnett, general manager and program director at WRNW in Briarcliff Manor (in Westchester County). This would have been an ideal opportunity for Howard, as he could pursue his career while remaining near Alison. But Stern did a most unexpected thing—he turned down the job. Overcome with misgivings, insecurities, and dark suspicions of his own inadequacies, Stern retreated from radio. In *Private Parts*, Stern recalls, "I freaked out. I got real nervous that I wasn't good enough." So he worked briefly in advertising, followed by a short stint selling radio time. The man who would be King of All Media was miserable. Alison urged Howard to follow up on the $96-a-week offer made by WRNW. Stern called Barnett.

Although the position that Barnett had originally called Stern about had already been filled, Barnett needed some-

At twenty-two, Stern was responsible for the midday shift at WRNW, known as Stereo 107. Although broadcast throughout the New York radio market, the station was little more than a few rooms in a house renovated into a cramped radio station with a meager three-thousand-watt signal, as opposed to the fifty-thousand-watt WNBC in Manhattan, which could be heard well beyond the five boroughs.

The bucolic setting was seemingly celebrated by the station, which advertised itself as "Progressive Rock from the Woods." Located in the boondocks of Westchester County, WRNW clearly fell short of Stern's metropolitan ambitions. On the other hand, it permitted him to explore his creativity and seek an individual voice—a distinctive radio persona.

Timid at first, Stern began to gain confidence and to experiment. Commercial spots were the primary outlets for Stern's comedic invention and exploration. While running

"My life is sincerely about envisioning a guy driving to work in his car and making him laugh."

body to cover him for the morning shift on a holiday. He had a scheduling conflict, having previously committed to work as a part-time disc jockey at WKTU, and Stern was the only person he could find to fill in. (Ironically, WKTU was formerly WHOM—where Ben Stern had worked briefly as a technician after World War II—and was destined to become WXRK, Howard's current radio home.) No promise of permanent employment was made at the time, but Stern was getting a chance to prove himself. He proved to be a bit of a fool.

A few minutes into Stern's show, the microphone jammed in the open position, sending every studio fumble and misstep onto the airwaves. With all studio sounds being broadcast, Stern was prevented from cuing up records. Compounding mistake upon mistake, the panicked Stern was hideously embarrassed and convinced that his days were numbered—to one. Eventually the chief engineer was called to the rescue and restored the studio to proper working condition. Stern apologized profusely for his gaggle of gaffs and was kept on by the station manager. Despite his disastrous debut, Stern was responsible: he was punctual, had a first-class radio license, and (in contrast to his future famously hirsute countenance) had respectably short hair. So Stern was offered a permanent position.

through their spots, Stern often contacted the sponsors by telephone and put them on the air. For years, disc jockeys had vigorously pitched their advertisers' products, but Stern was attempting to move things into a new dimension by not only pushing the product, but by personalizing the spots and making his shtick an intrinsic part of the commercial pitch. WRNW allowed him the latitude to alter the stale format of station IDs, time checks, news, weather, and disc spinning. For Stern, breaking the rules was not an act of arbitrary rebellion sparked by a rock and roll sensibility, but a calculated maneuver to carve a niche for himself. After all, there was no shortage of antic disc jockeys employing tired shtick. Stern aimed to surpass these plebeian personalities and create a league of his own.

In his junior year at B.U., Stern was clear on how he would become a standout in an endless field of insipid broadcasting clones. In an interview with *The Improper Bostonian*, Ellen Fruchtman remembered: "He used to talk about how he really needed to do something different. That he really needed to make a difference, but that if he didn't do something different, he would just be another dumb jock, making $16,000 a year forever. So he knew then, he really did, that he needed to do something outrageous."

**Previous page (inset):** Heavyset but not yet a media heavyweight, Stern entertains New Yorkers from his WNBC radio home.

"On my show it's kind of like, 'Well, I'll just be as stupid as I want to be.'"

Stern broadcasts to his Los Angeles radio audience on 97.1 KLSX.

An unshaven Stern promises

Los Angelenos unforgettable radio.

Stern may have been off-the-wall at WRNW but he was still a long way from "outrageous." Happily, the sponsors tended to respond favorably to Stern's personalized take on their ad copy. Emboldened, he soon began to incorporate impromptu exchanges with whomever may have been passing through the studio into his show while he was on the air. Stern had made an important discovery that would help define his comic approach in the years to come: he was at his best when riffing with other people.

## From Progressive to Regressive

In the fall of 1977, WRNW was sold and the new owners drastically reorganized the station's personnel. Barnett, the program director responsible for hiring Stern, was ousted. The sales manager, Yube Levin, whom Stern thought to be somewhat cocky and overconfident, was promoted to general manager. After a few more internal shuffles, Levin offered Stern the position of program director, which he accepted with one proviso: that he be allowed to maintain an on-air shift. Levin, who was hardly shy and anything but subtle, was of the opinion that Stern was without talent, had no future as a disc jockey, and had no business being on the radio. But Stern held his ground and Levin gave in. It was a small concession on Levin's part, for he was able to use the well-liked and malleable Stern for his own purposes of revamping the station.

The arrangement proved better financially for Stern: his salary increased from $4 an hour to $12,000 a year. Levin wanted to eliminate the progressive rock format of the station and move into the more homogenous sound of Top 40 radio. With his new program director's compliance, Levin gave the station a more lucrative, less imaginative format. Yes, Stern, the future Bane of All Management, acquiesced to the shortsighted, affronting Levin. But his obedience was most likely caused by nothing more than indifference. Following Levin's directive to purge old records and settle on a playlist of fifty records hardly fazed Stern, who "couldn't give a shit about the music." So unconcerned was he with musical content that Stern hired a "music director" and delegated the task of selecting records to him.

Meanwhile, Howard and Alison's relationship had blossomed. Alison was nearing the completion of her degree in social work and Howard was earning a modest salary. Wedding arrangements were made by the eager twenty-four-year-old lovebirds. On June 4, 1978, Alison and Howard were married at Temple Ohabei Shalom in Brookline, Massachusetts.

WRNW management appreciated their readily tractable program director, but Stern was growing uncomfortable in his role as a company man. Stern had proven himself a capable and cooperative employee but found himself nowhere nearer the radio personality he had hoped to become. The opportunity just wasn't there. Ultimately, Stern's hand was forced when Levin required him to demonstrate his managerial mettle by firing a fellow employee. Certain that he no longer wanted to work as management, Stern refused and began looking elsewhere for a job in radio. The decision was a good one. Clearly, his various duties at the station had only served to hinder his endeavors to originate a definitive on-air identity. Stern was determined to become a wild and crazy morning radio personality, but he had yet to accomplish anything truly outrageous in radio.

Stern was apprised that radio station WCCC, located in Hartford, Connecticut, was seeking the "wacky morning man" he hoped to become. Stern recalls that the audition tape he sent WCCC, which relied heavily on selections from comedy albums by Robert Klein and Cheech and Chong with interstitial one-liners penned by Stern, was hardly bursting with original comic invention. Stern forwarded the tape to WCCC's program director, Bill Nosal, who was suitably unimpressed. The not-yet-wacky Stern persevered and succeeded in coercing Nosal to grant him an interview. Both Stern and Nosal concur that Stern's first audition tape lacked any glimmer of inspiration or excitement. Prior to his future coronation as King of All Media, Stern reigned as Prince of Second Chances. Nosal consented to allow the ostensibly mediocre jock another audition. Stern surpassed his previous effort and won the job.

At fifty thousand watts, WCCC was quite a step up from WRNW. Financially, the position offered no advance—Stern was still making a paltry $12,000 per year. Fiscal security in mind, Alison maintained her job as a social worker in New York. Stern was forced to endure greater rigors at WCCC. His show hit the airwaves at 6 A.M. During his four-hour shift, he was responsible for just about everything that went on in the

# Higher or Lower Consciousness?

In 1957, Maharishi Mahesh Yogi founded the transcendental meditation program and the worldwide "spiritual regeneration movement," which purportedly "benefits all areas of an individual's life: mind, body, behavior, and environment." TM seeks to put the practitioner in touch with his or her true self via transcendental consciousness. This is defined as a state of restful alertness brought about by the chanting of a personal mantra for a period of fifteen to twenty minutes twice a day, while sitting in a relaxed position with one's eyes closed. TM became a staple of Stern's daily routine during his stint at WRNW, with sessions before and after broadcasts. Comparing the claims of the Maharishi Vedic Education Development Corp. with a cursory analysis of his apparent consciousness may help determine if Stern is a fully evolved Yogi Bear (his favorite cartoon as a child) or simply full of Yogi Bull.

CLAIM: TM groups score significantly higher on figural originality and flexibility and on verbal fluency.
FACT: The verbose and fluid Stern regularly appraises the physical attributes of sundry female figures, suggesting sexual positions that would certainly require a degree of "flexibility."
GRADE: Yogi Bear.
CLAIM: TM participants note that job performance and job satisfaction increase while desire to change jobs decreases. Significant improvements in relations with supervisors and coworkers are made.
FACT: Before landing at WXRK, Stern moved from city to city looking for the ideal situation. Stern has been known to alienate and even enrage members of his radio family and infuriate upper management. In *Playboy*, Stern proclaimed, "Radio is a scuzzy, bastard industry that's filled with deviants, circus clown rejects, the lowest of the low."
GRADE: Yogi Bull.
CLAIM: TM reduces tobacco, alcohol, and illicit drug use.
FACT: Stern is a teetotaler who hasn't done drugs since college.
GRADE: Yogi Bear.
CLAIM: TM participants develop a more strongly defined self-concept and come to perceive their "actual self" as significantly closer to their "ideal self."
FACT: Stern's self-deprecation is near legendary. He confided in *The New Yorker*, "I always feel like I'm garbage."
GRADE: Yogi Bull.
CLAIM: TM significantly improves overall physical health and mental well-being.
FACT: Stern suffered an obsessive-compulsive disorder for nearly two decades and was greatly debilitated by back pain. He attributes his cure to Dr. John Sarno, not TM.
GRADE: Yogi Bull.

On occasion, Stern has indicated that were he to give up radio he might consider moving to Iowa so as to be near one of the major TM centers. It's doubtful Stern will make such a move anytime soon. As a TM practitioner, Stern has masterfully brought transcendental consciousness, "a self-referral state of consciousness," into the realm of his radio persona, for the theme of any Howard Stern show, no matter what the topic, is always HOWARD STERN.

*"I represent maybe the crudest form of a man's sense of humor, but that's what guys like. That's what they laugh at."*

studio, including such broadcast minutiae as logging the precise time commercials were run and conducting the FCC requisite measurement of the station's transmitter output. When 10 A.M. rolled around, the "wild, fun morning guy" was required to perform a host of additional tasks such as producing commercials and preparing taped interviews. In *Private Parts*, Stern comments, "It was just an unbelievably exhausting job. There was no way to explain how bad it was."

## Surpassing Gas

As bad as it was, Stern began to come into his own during his tenure at WCCC. His efforts to shine in the wacky morning man franchise included an on-air "cadaverathon," in which he sought pledges of fresh cadavers to stock up Harvard and Yale medical schools' low supply of research specimens; wheedling State Senate Minority Leader Joseph I. Lieberman (whom Stern's memoirs designate "Majority Leader") to bestow his imprimatur upon an "official" document commemorating January 12 (Stern's birthday) "for the rest of eternity"; and telephoning Japan, where Paul McCartney had been busted for marijuana possession, to protest the former Beatle's incarceration. Stern's fairly revolutionary radio fare went essentially unnoticed until, quite by accident, he stumbled into notoriety.

In the midst of the gas crisis of 1979, the future media icon reached out and began to touch his audience—Stern was not yet brazen enough to fondle them. Stern encouraged his listeners to call in and respond to a chain letter that urged a boycott of Shell. The letter, which had been circulating throughout Hartford, touched a nerve with Stern, so he constructed a bandwagon onto which his angry listeners could jump. To demonstratively protest the higher prices and rationed supplies, Stern told his listeners to drive with their lights on during the day. Combining the spirit of political activist Jesse Jackson with the literary stylings of Dr. Seuss,

Stern "bottoms out" at the MTV Music Video Awards as Fartman.

Stern devised rhyming battle calls, such as "Turn the lights on bright until they get the prices right" and the more memorable, for brevity and specificity of target, "To hell with Shell!" The campaign was a success. No, the oil industry did not offer a shamefaced apology and promise to lower gas prices, but Stern did draw some highly visible media attention, which was surely his intent from the start.

The "To Hell with Shell" campaign, which lasted for all of two days, caused the press to pay attention to the upstart disc jockey and listeners to tune in, as indicated by WCCC's modest ratings surge during Stern's morning broadcast. Furthermore, a tape of Stern's show had come to the attention of Dwight Douglas, a radio consultant at Burkhart/Abrams & Associates. Douglas recalls: "I listened to the tape and I thought, there's something here. There's something going on. So, I called Howard Stern and asked him to give me a complete package and he was very efficient and after listening to the tape it struck me that he was kind of like Alan Alda on acid. And we recommended him for our station in Detroit, WWWW, which was referred to at that time as W-4."

There is some discrepancy in the accounts pertaining to Stern's initial contact with WWWW. Stern recalls contacting the station directly while Douglas lays claim to having forwarded Stern's tapes to Detroit. Paul D. Colford suggests that a more devious plot was afoot to remove Stern from Hartford's radio scene by rival station WHCN. Colford's investigation reveals that WHCN was responsible for originally providing Douglas with a tape of the rival station's jock's show, unbeknownst to Stern. WHCN's behind-the-scenes machinations were designed to compel the radio consultant to find Stern a position in another radio market.

No matter how the tapes made it to Detroit, WWWW's program director, Dick Huntgate, and general manager, Wally Clark, liked what they heard. Stern appeared to be the personality that could jump-start WWWW's broadcast engine and get their Motor City station cruising upward in the ratings. Stern was offered the job. Huntgate and Clark flew into Hartford to meet their future morning man and officially offer an annual salary of $28,000. Stern shared the news with Alison (who until that moment was unaware that her husband was courting a station in another city), his

father, and WCCC's owner, Sy Dresner, who evidently refused to make a counteroffer. A little negotiation, a bump to $30,000, and Stern was on his way to be Motown's morning man.

## Music, Mayhem, and Motown

As the 1970s came to an end, the United States was suffering through a host of problems, both domestically and internationally. Hostages were being held in Iran, President Jimmy Carter had lost the public's favor, and Detroit's auto industry was plagued with economic difficulties. Into this scene entered the new wacky morning guy. His work cut

# The "King of All Media" Meets the "King of Mars"

While employed by WCCC, Stern became acquainted with Fred Norris. Born Fred Leo Nukis (he legally changed his name to Eric Fred Norris in 1993) to Latvian immigrants on July 9, 1955, Norris grew up in Connecticut. In 1979, he was attending Western Connecticut State University during the day and working as the graveyard shift (midnight to 6 A.M.) disc jockey at WCCC. Norris' exhausting schedule, which seemed to preclude any opportunity for sleep, combined with his enigmatic demeanor caused Stern to conjecture that the overnight disc jockey was not of this world, possibly extraterrestrial—hence the nicknames "Earth Dog" Norris, "Frightening Fred," and the "King of Mars."

Early in their association, Stern and Norris collaborated on a number of comic bits that took advantage of Norris' talent for impersonations. He did Richard Nixon, Howard Cosell, Clint Eastwood, and Kurt Waldheim, Jr., to name but a few. Stern regularly acknowledges Norris' generous contributions to his career, especially in the early days. Primarily, he thanks Norris for filing his records away at WCCC, a chore the overworked Stern couldn't bring himself to complete. In *Miss America*, Stern praises Norris' selflessness in helping him to succeed.

Norris asserts, "To me comedy is hostility. Henny Youngman says, 'Take my wife, please.' I say, 'Take my wife, please—and while you're at it, stick a coat hanger up her nose.'" For Norris everyone is fair game, and empathy for those who may be offended only stands in the way of his making a living. He concedes, however, "There's a lot of things that run through my mind that would never get on the air." With such similarly twisted comic sensibilities, Norris and Stern make great counterparts.

Currently, Norris enjoys a place in the Stern radio family as a regular contributor of song parodies, sound effects, and impersonations as well as a participant in the daily radio show. Robin Quivers has said of Norris, "He's really off-center and he brings that special sense of weirdness to the show."

out for him, Stern would have to transport his listeners from their dire, dreary daily grind.

Stern's predecessor at WWWW, Steve Dahl, had moved on to Chicago and national fame by lamely seizing the "Disco Sucks" platform and campaigning to detonate a small mountain of disco albums at Comiskey Park. The explosive event, held between games at a twilight doubleheader, effected a melee that forced the White Sox to forfeit the second game. Dahl's antics were rabble-rousing crowd pleasers, and Stern was determined to surpass Dahl's popularity.

It became readily apparent that Stern had wandered into a less than ideal situation. The radio station described by Stern as "a bombed-out old house" and "a toilet bowl" (one of Stern's favorite metaphors) was foundering and the competition was threatening to bury the unstable station in the ratings. Nonetheless, Stern knew that whatever he accomplished at his new home would be potentially decisive in his future radio career. He had proven himself in Hartford; now Stern had to conquer an entirely new, unknown city. It wasn't going to be easy—it wasn't going to happen. Stern ventured to Detroit by himself, as Alison was required to give a month's notice to her job.

Stern attacked the airwaves with a vengeance, pulling out virtually all the stops. He began to explore the type of no-holds-barred radio he would perfect in the future. In comic response to the depressed economic climate, civic-minded Stern held cash giveaway contests—the windfall being limited to his pocket change. He orchestrated an event in which listeners donated money to destroy a Japanese car, the proceeds of which went to an American automobile manufacturer. On "Go Back to Bed Day," Stern coerced local employers to send a fortunate worker home for the day—with pay. Stern's material, increasingly unconventional, was still relatively tame. That was about to change.

Stern acknowledges that while he was working in Detroit, he experienced a revelation of sorts regarding honesty and ego. Ego stood in the way of his speaking truthfully to his audience and Stern aspired to unfettered, unedited honesty. Having roughly escorted his ego to the sidelines of consciousness, Stern's id burst onto the playing field. Stern regularly featured Irene the Leather Weatherlady, a local dominatrix, on his program. She was encouraged to impart a sadomasochistic, sexual frisson to her weather forecasts. In

Stern's own words, "I did anything to get noticed," including interviewing prostitutes, hosting Dial-a-Date segments featuring bodacious *Penthouse* pets wrestling other women, and having female impersonators impersonate celebrities on the station's front lawn. Stern had set two major trains of thought on a collision course in his seemingly one-track mind. With the impact of radio and sex, Stern personally endeavored to derail the radio industry while making a name for himself, but he was about to be railroaded right out of town.

## Git Along Urban Cowboy

Stern's ultimate failure to reign supreme on Detroit radio can be attributed mostly to WWWW's lack of focus and desperate attempts to gain a wider audience. In truth, Stern's ratings were lackluster at best, while the competitors had nearly triple the audience share he had in late 1980. But the newcomer was hardly being given a chance to break through. WWWW required that their morning man participate in any number of idiotic promotional events, none of which was in sync with Stern's on-air personality or interests. Audiences at these promotions were habitually indifferent to Stern, or worse, physically and verbally abusive. Stern feared that his presence at these outings, in addition to being downright unpleasant, bespoke his status as a potentially endangered subspecies. He dreaded the idea of becoming a part of the "lowlife" dominion of "circus clown rejects," has-beens, and never-wases that peopled the radio industry.

During his nine-month stint at WWWW, Stern had roughly hewn the format and further conceptualized his future radio show. There would be more chatter, less music, and greater interplay between Stern and a contingent of offbeat companions. Ironically, Stern, who dressed the part of a rock and roller while remaining persistently dispassionate about music (provocative comedy was his main focus), was decreed best album-oriented rock disc jockey by *Billboard* magazine while at WWWW. Not caring about the music was one thing, but later that year, when WWWW changed its format to country music practically overnight, the handwriting was on the wall—it was time to move on again.

Stern headed to the newsstand for a copy of *Radio & Records* (the very same radio industry trade publication that had alerted Stern to the job opening at WCCC in Hartford) and scanned the employment listings. Shortly thereafter, he received a job offer from WWDC, a station in Washington, D.C., popularly known as DC-101. Once again, pulling the strings behind the scenes was radio consultant extraordinaire, Dwight Douglas. Douglas had been in regular contact with DC-101's general manager, Godfrey "Goff" Lebhar, and championed Stern as the right man to blast off the station's daily broadcast. Lebhar was prepared to offer Stern only $40,000 a year, which was $10,000 less than his ending salary at WWWW. But eager to escape the downward spiral of the Detroit radio scene and gain closer proximity to his ultimate goal, New York, Stern accepted the offer and relocated to the nation's capital.

## Capitalizing

Stern arrived in Washington, D.C., with a clear vision for his radio show and a focus that would rival the most perspicacious voyeur's telescope. All barriers were to be destroyed, the competition was to be brought to its knees, and Stern would let loose the deluge of his torrent of consciousness. Stern was looking for a newsperson to come aboard who would do more than dutifully read the AP news feed, ideally somebody with a sense of humor. Stern knew that the topicality of the daily newscast would provide a treasure trove of comic material.

DC-101's program director, Denise Oliver, played a tape of Baltimore newscaster Robin Quivers for Stern, who was favorably impressed. Oliver proceeded to woo Quivers to work with Stern. Having only heard tapes of Stern's show and spoken with him via telephone, Quivers "lost all reservations" and signed on at DC-101. She remembers taking the job "just to meet" Stern. Call it kismet, serendipity, or just reckless abandon—Quivers' decision to work with Stern enhanced both their careers.

The configuration of DC-101's studio required Quivers to be secluded in a glassed-in booth behind Stern when she delivered her news broadcasts. Pleased with the facility of their on-air interaction, despite the obstacle of not being able to easily address one another eye to eye,

(continued on page 32)

# Quivering with Laughter

In March 1981, Robin Ophelia Quivers went on the air for the first time with Howard Stern. Stern professes that he knew Quivers was the "simpatico" radio partner he had sought from day one. A native of Baltimore, Quivers attended the University of Maryland, studied nursing, and served as a captain in the U.S. Air Force. Before teaming up with Stern, Quivers was working as a newsreader at WFBR-AM in Baltimore.

Quivers' role on Stern's radio show has steadily increased with the passing years. Initially a newsreader, Quivers has advanced to the position of Stern's number one sidekick and cohost. Stern readily acknowledges that Quivers' contribution to the show equals his and has indicated (perhaps erroneously) that airtime is split evenly between the two. Quivers brings a quick wit, sparkling, genuine laughter, and an ever present voice of reason to Stern's daily rambling radio show.

For years, the apparently upbeat Quivers was reticent to discuss various aspects of her past on the air, presumably because personal revelations were Stern's stock-in-trade. But in her 1995 autobiography, *Quivers: A Life*, the silence was broken and Stern's cohort dropped a bombshell. Quivers revealed an unhappy childhood in which she suffered sexual abuse by her father and a resultant history of mental anguish, emotional volatility, and necessary psychotherapy.

Occasionally, Quivers, who is black, is reprimanded by those legions who would enforce political correctness for sitting by idly while Stern engages in sometimes caustic ethnic humor. Stern has been accused of cannily selecting Quivers to use as a shield for deflecting criticism of his racial humor. This patently absurd position is demeaning to Quivers. Those who want Quivers to "take the black view" reduce her to the stereotype they supposedly revile. Why should Quivers assume a point of view based on color? Surely her critics would be horrified at the notion that all black people think alike. Stern contests that apart from not knowing Quivers was black when he first heard her tape, he chose the best possible person as his sidekick: "I don't give a fuck what color they are as long as they're talented."

Stern insisted that Quivers become more involved throughout the show. In Quivers, Stern had found the ideal partner off whom he could bounce material—on the air! Stern's brilliant innovation was to go into the studio unrehearsed and improvise. This was a vital and exciting radio revolution, especially when compared to the spate of overly rehearsed jocks offering prerecorded material to a bored public.

Quivers was a crucial component in this approach to morning radio. Initially her goal was to be a serious newscaster, heard by as many listeners as possible; an association with the controversial morning man was her passport to notoriety. But on Stern's show, Quivers was to do more than just read the news. By Stern's request, Quivers kept her microphone open throughout the show and responded naturally to whatever went on in the studio. For the maverick morning team, things were moving along nicely...until the station's management descended.

## Mr. and Mismanagement

Stern's previous experience had prepared him for the inevitability of managerial myopia, but he hadn't anticipated its extent. Denise Oliver, the intermediary who had the foresight to broker the combination of Stern and Quivers, frequently sought to undermine the newly conjoined duo's easy rapport in her role as program manager. Evidently oblivious to the magnetizing chemistry between Stern and Quivers, Oliver endeavored to stifle their interaction. First, Oliver directed Quivers to cease conversing with Stern on the air and instructed her to actively prevent Stern from interrupting the newscast. Fortunately, both Stern and Quivers knew that such commandments were sheer stupidity. To terminate the genial duet's discourse was to tear the soul out of Stern's morning show. Despite Oliver's mandate, Stern and Quivers retained their on-air dialogue. The

"Robin has a great laugh, and that laugh is one of the reasons I love her. It gets you talking. She's a facilitator. She instigates."

gauntlet had been thrown; Stern's skirmishes in his war with management were just beginning.

Oliver worked to tighten the reins on Stern the warhorse. The spontaneity that provided Stern's show with its unique feel was challenged by management. In their efforts to control Stern, the radio station strove to impose a restrictive format on his show. Instead of allowing Stern to pursue his free-form approach to radio, Oliver and company sought to channel his material into a rigid schedule. Attempts to compartmentalize the show were doomed to failure: Stern would not commit to a schedule in which certain bits were to air at specific times on particular days of the week. Soon, Stern would deliver positive proof of the merit of his method.

By the summer of 1981, Stern achieved a nearly miraculous increase in audience share, having more than doubled his ratings. Confronted with Stern's fantastic numbers, management backed off—he must have been doing *something* right. Oliver's meddling ceased altogether that September, when she was succeeded as program director by Don Davis. Stern seized the opportunity to assault his boss, general manager Goff Lebhar. If Stern had a bone to pick with his perceived enemy, he would not stop until the offending person was thoroughly excoriated.

Stern describes Lebhar as "the biggest pain in the ass I ever worked for" prior to his days at NBC. On the air Stern would mock Lebhar, whom he would deride as "Goof Le Phoof," and adopted a position that he would constantly revisit—namely, that management was comprised of small-minded oppressors who lacked appreciation for the underpaid Stern. Presumably Lebhar tolerated Stern's

*(continued on page 36)*

**Left:** Quivers arrives at Brentano's Books in New York City for a book signing wearing a sparkling outfit to match her on-air personality. **Following pages:** Stern and the gang re-create the radio show magic in a scene from *Private Parts*. From left to right: Norris, Jackie "the Joke Man" Martling, Stern, Quivers.

insubordination because his morning man was a cash cow. Sponsors paid big money to advertise on Stern's show; Stern deserved appropriate remuneration.

Stern was signed on with DC-101 until the end of July 1982, and in lieu of renegotiating his contract with the tightfisted Lebhar, he campaigned for some much needed assistance in the studio. The candidate Stern chose for this position was none other than his former colleague from his Hartford days, Fred Norris. Lebhar accepted Stern's demands. With Norris on the team, Stern's show moved to the next level. In addition to attending to a variety of production needs, Norris conspired with Stern to create a juggernaut of savage comedy.

The radio entourage was augmented by what Stern called his "Think Tank." The assembled minds were less Albert Einstein and more Alfred E. Neuman (Stern was an avid *Mad Magazine* reader). These were regular guys just chewing the fat, not for fame or fortune (they received no pay) but for fun. The Think Tank consisted of lawyer Harry Cole, record store manager Steve Kyger, and salesman (later a radio executive) Steve Chaconas. On-air conversations among the Think Tank were moderated by Stern, who acted as participant and director, editing on the fly. Off the air the Think Tank submitted ideas for bits and offered potential discussion topics. In an interview, Chaconas recalled:

"We never knew when the mikes were on. We would sit there and Howard would start talking about something and I'd have to ask people, 'Well, how was the show today, what did we talk about?' And they would say, 'Oh, you guys were doing this,' and I had no idea we were on the air. We had mikes there, it was like a bunch of guys hangin' out, just shootin' the breeze and having a good time and Howard would throw up a topic, someone else would throw up a topic and we'd end up going with it."

The easygoing, impromptu nature of the Think Tank's interactions encouraged Stern to pursue a more-talk and, in time, all-talk format. However, DC-101 was putatively a rock station, and much to Davis' consternation, Stern was playing less music.

Washingtonians tuned in to DC-101 in record numbers to hear what Stern and his gang would do next. Stern regularly

fought with management for permission to expand the show's boundaries. Audiences were treated to (or offended by) "Beaver Breaks," twisted spoofs in which the characters from television's squeaky clean *Leave it to Beaver* were dragged through the mud; Gay Dial-a-Date; and rank-out contests. The popularity of his incursions into sketch comedy encouraged Stern to release an album. Named after the title song, "50 Ways to Rank Your Mother" (a parody of Paul Simon's "50 Ways to Leave Your Lover"), which was written by Think Tank member Harry Cole, the album featured new recordings of pieces culled from the radio show. Stern appeared on the album cover dressed in boots and leather, brandishing a whip above a maternal figure cowered to her knees. Curiously, Stern's "half-Christian" name is spelled "Howeird" on the record cover. Washington fans lined up around the block when Stern made a public appearance to sign copies of the record upon its release. The rights to the album changed hands and the record was rereleased by Citizen X/Ichiban Records in 1994 as *Unclean Beaver*.

A judgmental press conferred upon Stern the title "Shock Jock." Stern, who believes the label to be misleading, avows that his intent has never been to shock but to entertain. Nonetheless, Stern's time in Washington is best remembered for two notorious broadcasts in 1982 that stirred up considerable emotions.

Stern's first victim was Alison, who was pregnant. Early in her first trimester, Alison suffered a miscarriage. Stern responded to the tragedy by joking about it on the air. The insensitivity of Stern's japes horrified much of his female audience as well as Alison, who hadn't listened to the broadcast and learned of her husband's cruel comedy secondhand. A local reporter contacted the Stern household, presumably to get Alison's response, and regaled her with the details of the show. The theretofore oblivious Alison became infuriated. Stern apologized. This marked a critical point in the newlywed couple's relationship, for it was apparent that Stern would continue to mine their personal life for material. Nothing was off limits. In *Private Parts*, Alison admits that she felt "violated," "mortified," and "betrayed" by her husband's public mockery of their very private tragedy. Despite her fury at the time, she indicates an inability to "stay mad at Howard," and remarks, "I know this sounds corny, but he can turn to me and say, 'I didn't really mean to hurt you, I really love you,' and then it's all over with." Forgiveness aside, Alison admits, "I still get angry when he talks about our personal life, even to this day."

In the winter, an Air Florida flight plummeted into the Fourteenth Street Bridge on the Potomac River near Washington. Failure to de-ice the wings caused the deadly crash. Infuriated by the negligence of the airline, Stern pretended to telephone Air Florida and inquire about the price of "a one-way ticket from National to the Fourteenth Street Bridge." The magnitude of the event horrified some listeners and affected the public's perception of Stern's biting satire. It was even incorrectly reported that this was the reason for Stern's eventual dismissal from DC-101. Years later Stern

*"I think that if you are happy and healthy and complacent, you're not funny."*

still found himself attempting to clarify the facts involved in the now legendary incident.

Actually, Stern's departure from Washington radio had more to do with an inadequate salary and an increasing disdain for Lebhar than it did with his listeners' reactions. In *Private Parts*, Stern recounts that Lebhar felt he deserved to share the accolades afforded the popular morning man for having turned the station around. Absurdly, Lebhar believed the press should mention his role in DC-101's success story. Once again, Stern knew that it was time to move on and began to covertly seek work elsewhere. Stern hastened his demise at DC-101 by grumbling about his salary ($84,000 a year) on-air and announcing that Lebhar earned $364,000 a year. Stern had gone too far. He was finished at DC-101.

Expelled from the nation's capital, Stern was on his way to a job in the city in which he had always wanted to work: New York. He had finally realized his childhood dream...but the nightmare was about to begin.

**Opposite:** Stern's "constantly attentive, totally overbearing," and loving mother, Ray. **Above:** Stern, looking dapper in a suit, leads the way for his wife.

"They'll say, 'You can't use that—don't discuss on the air what we've just said.' But I have to."

# CHAPTER THREE

# Bite the Big Apple

DC-101 fired their popular morning man (Stern was named best disc jockey by *Washingtonian Magazine*) months before his contract expired, but Stern had already concluded negotiations with WNBC-AM in New York. Stern was enticed by the financially attractive deal (approximately $200,000 a year), but he would be moving to New York radio alone—WNBC had no interest in Quivers or Norris.

Quivers was furious at Stern for deserting his radio family. She was offered a continuing position at DC-101, but she declined and became a reporter for WCBM-AM in Baltimore. Norris hung on at DC-101. Stern insists that he had every intention of persuading WNBC management to hire Quivers and Norris once he was established at the station. He was in for a fight: once again, management would prove to be at odds with their new employee.

Approximately one month before Stern took over the 4-to-8 P.M. shift at WNBC, he was confronted by an unexpected attacker. *NBC Magazine*, the network's television magazine, broadcast a most unflattering portrait of the Shock Jock in a segment titled "X-Rated Radio." This exercise in journalistic character assassination was hosted by reporter Douglas Kiker, the Washington correspondent for *NBC Magazine*, who sat in front of a background graphic of a portable radio with the word "family" emblazoned upon an oval in the lower right. Kiker proclaimed: "What you are about to hear is going to shock and disgust you, because it's vulgar, even obscene. A warning: if there are any children in the room you might not want them to watch this report. It's X-rated radio, barnyard radio, and there's more and more of it on the air because kids love it."

Kiker filed this report from his home in the capital city. The segment featured a variety of visually and verbally manipulative ploys. Kiker, holding his child on his lap, turned off the radio broadcasting Stern's show in disgust and lamented that, in spite of the many precautions to defend his home from outside intrusion (window and door locks, even an alarm system), Stern's sonic scourge has penetrated his heavily armored domicile. In a panel discussion, a "concerned parent" declares that "Vietnam at dinnertime was bad enough, but this stuff over my Cocoa Puffs is driving me crazy!" Evidently, Kiker and the panelists were unable to control the power switch on their home radios and preferred censorship over responsible parenting. Thus, a month prior to Stern's WNBC debut, the waters were already poisoned. WNBC brass took note of Kiker's piece and prepared to put the screws to their new disc jockey.

WNBC's designs to restrain their new unruly disc jockey with an iron fist should have come as no surprise. Separating Stern from his radio family was just the beginning of the divide-and-conquer campaign masterminded by NBC Radio's executive vice president, Robert Sherman. Sherman assured NBC executives that without his cohorts, Stern would be more vulnerable and easily managed.

Sherman had also brought Don Imus back to WNBC in 1979. A former uranium miner from Arizona, Imus was one of the original bad boys of radio and his morning show was hugely popular. But Imus' history of drug and alcohol abuse troubled management. Stern was essentially brought on to fill the afternoon drive-time slot, which was lagging in eleventh place, but would also serve as a backup should Imus' chemical problems keep him from performing his

**Previous page (inset):** Stern peers out quizzically from behind eyeglasses instead of his typical sunglasses. **Below:** Overweight, overwrought, and underappreciated, Stern suffers at AM radio station 66 "Double-U-*ENNN*-Bee-Cee!"

on-air duties. (During Imus' first stint at WNBC in 1973, alcohol had caused him to miss one hundred days of work.) Sherman avowed that Stern would "apply the coup de grace to the New York market." The network's executives were still wary of Stern but believed, with Sherman's assurance, that they could mold Stern into their image. Besides, it would have been extremely costly (around $500,000) for WNBC to get out of their contract. Thus, even before he began work at WNBC, precautions had already been taken to police Stern's show and revoke his creative license.

## A Virulent Strain

At WNBC, Stern entered a no-win situation guaranteed to make everyone unhappy. Cut off from his radio family and virtually forbidden from pursuing his own brand of material, Stern labored in misery. Regarding his early days at WNBC, Stern told *New York Magazine*, "I was crying, ready to kill myself. I thought I'd gotten myself in with the biggest bunch of idiots! How could they break up my act? I kept wondering why they hired me in the first place."

Set to the task of ruthlessly managing Stern was program director Kevin Metheny. The adversarial relationship between these two men would force Stern to descend to a new level—Metheny was going down. Years later, Metheny would recall thinking, "This is going to be different than I thought." Different was an understatement. The on-air insults Stern hurled at Lebhar were but mild jests compared to what he had in store for his new foe. Having identified the opposition, all Stern had to do was label the enemy. Something ugly would do.

"Pig Virus" was the unfortunate name by which Stern referred to Metheny in his on-air tirades against management. Primarily, Stern was aggravated by WNBC's efforts to reprogram—or perhaps deprogram—him while utterly controlling the content of his broadcasts. Attempts were made to soften the rough and cutting edges perceived in Stern's radio personality. WNBC wanted their "bad boy" to come across as a "nice guy." The station apparently coveted the financial rewards of an association with Stern but refused to accept the risk.

On-air damage control was sustained by Metheny, who regulated a "dump button." If Stern wandered into territory

Bad glasses, bad mustache, and bad management, Stern enjoys a lighter moment at WNBC.

considered offensive or questionable, Metheny would hit the button and kill the broadcast. Confused listeners would hear an abrupt cut from Stern's show to music or a commercial. This only served to rouse Stern's greater ire.

Metheny and the executives at WNBC were operating within the self-imposed limitations of their medium. Radio was about ratings, records, and regulations. Management was very old-school, less interested in their new disc jockey's unique personality than his adherence to pronouncing the station's call letters exactly the same as the rest of the on-air talent: "double-u-ENN-bee-cee!" Meanwhile, Imus, who was pulling in good ratings, was given greater creative leeway. WNBC gave Imus a hand while all Stern got was the finger. Stern responded by thumbing his prodigious nose.

Stern regularly defied a list of seven directives presented to him by WNBC general manager Domenick Fiorvanti. The septet of guidelines delineated those topics and themes about which Stern was forbidden to joke: personal tragedies, attacks on persons, sickness and death, sex, scatology, religion, and the "seven dirty words"—all of which, except the words, were integral to Stern's comedy.

If management had intended to tame Stern, this list of seven deadly radio transgressions only provoked him to go forth and sin some more. In fact, within one month at his new radio home, Stern was suspended for airing a sketch in which one of God's video games is unveiled. In a spoof of the wildly popular Donkey Kong, "God" presented "Virgin Mary Kong," in which Mary fights her way through a Jerusalem singles bar in an effort to avoid impregnation. WNBC's rules and standards seemed arbitrary. Imus was allowed to continue doing bits involving his character, the Right Reverend Dr. Billy Sol Hargis, and other "outrageous" sketches, but Stern was kicked off the air after one misstep. The inequity would breed contempt.

To the press, Stern maintained the pretense of being thrilled to be working at WNBC. He even went so far as to compliment Imus, but hastened to point out that the very reason WNBC hired him was because he was different and did not cop Imus' shtick like so many other disc jockeys. In truth, the restraints imposed upon Stern and the free rein afforded Imus would bring about bad blood between the bad boys. In the years to come, Imus would declare that Stern was "a dirty-mouthed little punk," who aspired to emulate his act; Stern would counter that Imus was "a drunken, over-the-hill bigot," who was merely ripping off his act. The United Nations would be hard-pressed to make peace between the two radio personalities, who have nothing but a lack of respect for each other to this day.

## Where There's Ill Will There's a Way

Stern's problematic debut in New York was exacerbated by his lack of on-air support. Fred Norris had finally been brought aboard to help with the comedy bits, sound effects, and other aspects of production, but Stern still lacked a verbal sparring partner. During the news segment of the show, straitlaced WNBC news reporter Neal Seavey either refused or was unable to banter with Stern. Without the lively interaction between Stern and his radio family, the show was hopelessly doomed to failure. This was abundantly clear to anyone listening in, and management, recognizing that the show lacked vitality, acquiesced to Stern's relentless requests and hired Robin Quivers. Stern had gone so far as to suggest that Quivers would be able to keep his outrageous antics and unruly behavior in check. In actuality, Quivers was uncertain if she ever wanted to work with Stern again. In her autobiography, Quivers recounts that this was a physically and psychologically devastating period and recollects that "Howard became the focus for all my rage." Ultimately, Stern and Quivers were able to "wipe the slate clean" and pick up where they left off. The radio family was reunited.

Fiorvanti and Metheny perceived a threat in Stern with his aides-de-camp and responded with authoritarian dictates. They would bend Stern to their will or break him. Stern was commanded to limit his speaking to two-and-a-half-minute intervals. When Stern exceeded his limit, Metheny, gesticulating wildly, would attempt to cut him off. In addition to using the dump button, Metheny would also turn off Stern's microphone. Metheny is even reported to have hurled a telephone at Stern during a broadcast.

In the aftermath of the *Miss Howard Stern New Year's Eve Pageant* pay-per-view extravaganza, Stern and Quivers address the press and make no apologies for the bad taste exhibited both on and off stage.

Adding to Stern's Orwellian nightmare, management created and posted propaganda where he worked. Former Think Tank panelist Steve Chaconas recalled, "When you walked into the studio at NBC, they had a collage of a family sitting down eating dinner together, people going to church and they had a big banner across the top saying 'Howard remember: This is your audience.'"

The barrage of assaults and restrictions was taking its toll on the radio team. Both Stern and Quivers put on about fifty pounds each. Stern recalled, "I was begging them to let me out of my contract but then something told me to shut up and wait them out—they'd leave first." It was the right decision.

About a year and a half into his stay at WNBC, Stern's listenership and ratings began to steadily increase. Despite all of management's attempts to squelch their unpredictable afternoon disc jockey, Stern had proven the validity of his approach to radio. The ratings vindicated his stubborn refusal to toe the party line and even Metheny would eventually concede, "As time went by, his program worked in spite of everything we'd believed. We've come to recognize that some radio personalities can be compelling enough to break the rules." Whether Stern had changed management's beliefs was less important than the simple fact that climbing ratings meant increased revenue.

## Viral Defection

Fortunately, when Randall D. Bongarten succeeded Fiorvanti as general manager in July 1983, the tables turned in Stern's favor. Metheny departed in January 1984 and was eventually replaced by a more easygoing program director, Dale Parsons. Bongarten represented a friendlier regime that afforded Stern, a relative unknown, freedom and respect. Under Bongarten's command, Stern's salary was doubled and bonus incentives were added to his contract. Additionally, Stern's show shifted to an improved 3-to-7 P.M. slot. Bongarten granted Stern dispensation to do his act and be himself. It is little wonder that Stern often referred to Bongarten as "one of the greatest people who ever lived" and his "savior."

Stern had other reasons to celebrate. A newborn daughter, Emily, now augmented the Stern household. In the years that would follow, the Shock Jock would offer listeners a glimpse into another facet of his personality—Stern the family man. Those who thought Stern a licentious, subhuman beast who merely paid lip service when professing to faithfully love his unfortunate wife were surprised by Stern's heartwarming expression of genuine affection for his little girl. When Alison telephoned the station, Stern had her put little Emily on the line. Any rants or raves would halt as Stern crooned a warbling testament of sincere paternal love to his precious child.

Stern was allowed to completely overturn the restrictive format imposed on him by Metheny and company. Bongarten knew that Stern would flourish with his newfound liberty. Stern was no longer required to spin a certain

## Less Music Is More

Stern outlasted the oppressive managerial regime of Metheny and Fiorvanti at WNBC. One may imagine that the practically unmanageable Stern was the reason for their departure, driving "Pig Virus" to his wits' end and generally irritating Fiorvanti. In truth, better employment opportunities arose for both executives. Fiorvanti moved on to become senior vice president and general manager of MTV (Music Television). Metheny (portrayed in the final frames of the film *Private Parts* as having degenerated into a raving, foul-mouthed lunatic) became vice president of VH-1 (Video Hits One).

During his time at WNBC, Stern increased the amount of talk on his show and played fewer and fewer records. Inasmuch as WNBC was struggling against FM competitors WPLJ and WHTZ in the Top 40 market, Stern's dismissive attitude toward playing music infuriated management. Additionally, Stern tended to broadcast his criticism, often unfavorable, of those discs he consented to spin.

The programming for MTV and VH-1 initially sought to offer music videos around the clock. Curiously, since the early 1990s, music videos have become less and less prevalent in the daily lineup. Also notable is the success of the cartoon *Beavis and Butt-head* on MTV, which embraces the spirit of Stern's radio show by ridiculing the very music it features.

number of records, and the free-form banter he had pioneered with his Washington Think Tank was back. Stern added writers Al Rosenberg and Jackie "the Joke Man" Martling to his staff as well as producer Gary Dell'Abate. Given carte blanche, Stern orchestrated the show at his own indiscretion. The public got to experience the full force of Stern's unleashed comic offensive. Stern delivered what his audience wanted: SEX.

## Tuned In and Turned On

In addition to bringing about a more relaxed atmosphere, Bongarten publicly exhibited an appreciation of Stern's value to the station. Measures were taken to eliminate the perceived schism between Imus and Stern, at least to the public eye. Previously, Imus was advertised as WNBC's reigning king of morning radio and Stern, by default, was the afternoon vassal. Although attempts were made to sell New Yorkers on the entire broadcast day (*Mad Magazine* artist Jack Davis illustrated subway posters for both Imus' and Stern's shows), "Imus in the morning" was a preeminent catchphrase in the majority of the station's advertising.

Bongarten sought to even the playing field and force his disc jockeys to work as teammates. The small advertising agency Penchina, Selkowitz, Inc. developed an amusing television advertising campaign that celebrated WNBC's outrageous on-air talents. However, bringing the temperamental Imus together with a relative newcomer whose youth and originality threatened the old-timer required extensive negotiations.

Research had revealed that WNBC's listeners seemed to enjoy being scandalized by Imus and Stern. High ratings indicated that there was a largely clandestine audience that tuned in but refused to confess its guilty pleasure. Imus evidently thought he was too good to be paired with Stern and directed his agent to make arrangements that would ensure the veteran shock jock more airtime than the upstart Stern. Even after an agreement had been reached, it was still up in the air as to whether Imus would show up for the shoot. When Imus finally appeared and refused to participate, Bongarten masterfully manipulated the situation and successfully provoked, rather than stroked,

Imus' bloated ego. It had been decided that if Imus would not cooperate, then the commercial would feature Stern alone. Imus knew better than to cede Stern the advantage of his absence and resigned himself to do the spot as planned.

The commercial, as it finally appeared on television, purported to be a televised apology by WNBC for its devilishly delinquent disc jockeys. At a news desk with "66 WNBC AM

*"People perceive me as Howard Stern. It's not the case. I'm Howard Stern with a vocabulary. I'm the man he wishes he could be."*

*—Don Imus*

**Right:** Jackie "the Joke Man" Martling, donning the fool's cap, plays court jester to the King of All Media. **Opposite:** A man of a million gags and dozens of hand gestures, *Jackie "the Joke Man" Martling.*

STEREO" looming large in the background, Bongarten, flanked by Imus and Stern, offered a mock apology to the offended masses, which included the mayor of New York, the Queen of England, and even Bongarten's wife. While Bongarten read his list, Imus maintained his swaggering demeanor of disregard while Stern pretended a level of moderate contrition. The commercial concluded with Imus pronouncing, over Bongarten's seemingly endless list, the station's number and call letters followed by the new slogan "If we weren't so bad, we wouldn't be so good."

The campaign was extremely popular, and posters featuring the commercial's tag line below pictures of Stern and Imus that were defaced, presumably by angry graffitist listeners, appeared throughout New York City. The image of Stern and Imus, who appear to be cozily sitting shoulder to shoulder, was a composite created from two separate photo shoots—it was best to keep the two stars apart from each other. Suddenly, the public had a face to go along with Stern's voice. Bongarten encouraged Stern to make other television appearances, such as on *Donahue* and *Late Night with David Letterman*. This added exposure, combined with the successful and pervasive advertisements, meant that Stern could no longer anonymously use the subway to return home from work. He rated a private car; management was all too happy to arrange for their star disc jockey's safe transport.

Stern appeared as a new breed, breaking ground while Imus seemed ready to be put out to pasture. In truth, Stern

**Left:** Looking more like "filthy thirds" than "sloppy seconds," Stern, in drag, promotes *Miss America* on *Late Night with David Letterman*. **Above:** Although Stern includes Phil Donahue in his list of "Celebrities Who Irritate Me," an opportunity to support the First Amendment while calling attention to his book, *Private Parts*, lured the radio personality/author into making an appearance on Donahue's show.

On the set of *Private Parts*, Stern and company are joined by rock and roll legends AC/DC.

was gradually surpassing Imus in ratings and popularity. Hoping that some of the Stern magic would rub off, Imus began to pay attention (even respect) to the newest star in the WNBC firmament. Previously Imus and his cohorts expressed nothing but disdain—to the point of utter disregard—for Stern and his show. Hoping to convert some of Stern's listeners to his own show, Imus began to drop by or phone in while Stern was on the air. It soon became clear that Imus felt threatened by Stern's wildly popular show and was hanging around with the intention of incorporating parts of the afternoon show into his morning slot.

Stern believed Imus was ripping off his act but viewed the older jock's execution of the material as pathetic and poorly done. Despite an uneasy truce, the tension between the two men made for entertaining radio. Stern would slam Imus and Imus would bite back. Because it was Stern's show, the length and extent of Imus' intrusions could be controlled, always giving Stern the upper hand and the last word.

Stern was in top form and his popularity was reflected in soaring ratings. Bongarten allowed great liberty and exhibited

## Gag Order

**Jackie "the Joke Man" Martling makes extensive and crucial contributions to Stern's daily comic output. Throughout the program, Martling incessantly scrawls gags and one-liners on scraps of paper that he passes to Stern, who readily incorporates the material into his ongoing spiel. Stern graciously acknowledges that he uses a high percentage (nearly 95 percent) of Martling's scribblings.**

**Martling, another Long Island native, is a graduate of Michigan State University with a degree in mechanical engineering. Before hooking up with Stern, Martling performed in the Long Island comedy circuit as part of a novelty rock act and, later, as a stand-up comic. Unlike the spate of contemporary, observational comics, Martling's act is reminiscent of old-time burlesque hall comedians. Audiences are assaulted with a nonstop barrage of off-color, decidedly politically incorrect material. In reference to Martling's comedy tape, *Sergeant Pecker*, Luigi Lucaire calculated Martling to exceed the "laugh a minute" paradigm by more than four times!**

**Martling is an industrious self-promoter and marketing master. In fact, Stern became aware of Martling through a mass mailing campaign in which Martling liberally distributed a homemade comedy tape. Initially, Martling's appearances were limited to bits such as "Stump the Comedian," but Stern soon recognized the comedian's value and brought him on as head writer. The volatile Martling generally feels underappreciated or put upon and regularly threatens to walk off the show. However, these thunderclouds soon evaporate as Stern's show offers the vigorously self-advertised gag man endless opportunities to plug his books, records, and club dates.**

What makes Stern's radio show so compelling is the sense that everything is up front and nothing is hidden. As evidenced in this scene from *Private Parts*, bodacious studio guests often join in this spirit of full disclosure.

his good nature when Stern would broadcast his ongoing "war" with management. On the rare occasion when Bongarten attempted to seize control, Stern called his wife and implored her to sexually satisfy her husband so as to improve his mood. Bongarten recalls a time when Stern went too far: "Howard was doing a bit on, 'Why don't Jewish women use their mouths for anything except eating Chinese food?' Now, we all know what Howard was talking about. And, you know, one point—I felt it was just a little bit more explicit than I would care for. And I got him, while he was on the air, and I said 'Howard, I, you know, you've got to stop this,' and he did. But he turned it into a bit of, 'Was I Right to Stop Him?'"

Stern remained true to form and transformed most of the behind-the-scenes aspects of his professional dealings into comic material he'd use on the show. He had discovered a formula that worked. By voicing his acrid grievances with management on the air, Stern appealed to those listeners who wanted to lash out at their onerous employers. He became a sort of hero to the persecuted proletariat. As Stern told an interviewer around this time: "I would say that most people talk the way I talk, think the way I think, and are a little bit inhibited because of the nature of the work they do or because (of) their families and their friends. They can't really loosen up, so I do it for 'em. I'm like a, I'm like a big piece of Ex-Lax in the afternoon. I loosen up for all the people who're out there who just want to break loose."

# The Incubus Emerges from Out of the Hayes

As good as things were for Stern at WNBC, they were about to get a whole lot worse. Bongarten's superior management abilities were required elsewhere in the organization and he was promoted to president of NBC Radio. Stern was losing his most sympathetic supporter. Bongarten's successor as general manager was John P. Hayes, Jr., whom Bongarten had recruited from an NBC-owned San Francisco station. Prior to Hayes' arrival at WNBC on October 1, 1984, Stern contacted the future general manager on the phone and instigated a fractious on-air exchange. Initially hanging up on Hayes for having kept him on hold, Stern subsequently contacted Hayes' secretary and categorized the ground rules by which Hayes was to abide when dealing with WNBC's number one on-air personality.

In interviews with the press, Hayes indicated that he was attuned to Stern's sense of humor and acknowledged that he fully anticipated becoming a target of Stern's invective. Although he professed to be inured to the rough-and-tumble world of rock and raunch radio, Hayes proved to have a thinner skin than he claimed. Whereas Bongarten was a willing foil who tacitly sanctioned the ongoing Stern-versus-management fracas, Hayes set out to willfully foil the hugely popular Stern. Stern would come to see Hayes as the demonic second coming of "Pig Virus." It was as if managerial swine flu had skipped a generation and mutated into a deadly new organism; Stern soon dubbed his new archenemy "the Incubus."

Following his first encounter with Hayes at WNBC, Stern went on-air to recount details of the meeting. Confiding with his radio family, Stern characterized Hayes as a "douche bag" and predicted that the new general manager would be "a pushover." He went on to predict that his show would get filthier. Stern's tactless tack was to slap Hayes in the face by way of throwing down the gauntlet. Bongarten understood that Stern's rude methods were part of the game, but Hayes was not playing. Naturally antiauthoritarian, Stern would not tolerate the officious, clean-cut Hayes and defiantly declared that he was unwilling to yield the right, or wrong, of way. Proper stewardship of Stern required that he be coaxed or cajoled, never commanded. Hayes would not coddle Stern and a war of wills and won'ts commenced.

Compulsive opposition to managerial mandates was Stern's modus operandi. That which was forbidden loomed before Stern like Everest above Sir Edmund Hillary. When asked why he continually did what he was asked not to do, Stern proclaimed, "Because it was there! When I'm on the radio, I just can't be muddled down with what I can't do." Disregarding Stern's succinct declarations, Hayes insisted on playing a Sherpa guide headed for the high road. Steps were taken to prevent Stern from going too far. The foolhardy Hayes offered to direct or modify Stern's humor and palliate potentially offensive material into something more palatable. In an interview with Jan Hoffman, Hayes remembered, "I used to meet with Howard and tell him, 'I trust you, you're responsible, but if you're thinking of something that's really outrageous, let me know and I'll figure out a way to do it.'" As far as Stern was concerned, all of Hayes' ideas were "lame" and therefore negligible.

Robin Quivers lends her signature laugh to the radio show in a scene from *Private Parts*.

What truly rankled Stern was the new general manager's idea of adding on-air personalities to WNBC's daily roster. Radio legend Wolfman Jack was brought in to work the overnight shift by late 1984. In mid-April 1985, veteran media personality Soupy Sales was installed in the time slot between Imus and Stern.

As a youth, Stern had admired the comic brilliance of the irreverent and anarchic Sales. Times had changed but Sales' material remained the same, his cutting edge duller than a timeworn butter knife. Not only was his gentle, out-of-date humor inconsistent with WNBC's bad boy lineup, but Stern's childhood idol had feet of clay that treaded heavily on the afternoon jock's toes. Furthermore, Stern resented management's unconditional respect for and expansiveness toward the newly arrived old-timer. Sales was granted extensive perks, including, among other things, a grand piano, a piano accompanist, additional staff, and limousine service. After three years at WNBC Stern seethed that he still had to share a fleet car with Quivers and Norris.

## Offensive as Opposed to Obnoxious

Clearly, Hayes preferred the lightweight, cornball brand of humor purveyed by Sales. Controlling Stern was tiresome and futile. Hayes professed that Stern, whom he acknowledged to be clever and naturally funny, often relied on material for shock value alone. Hayes continued to espouse his opinion that Stern occasionally crossed the line from merely obnoxious to offensive. In his interview with Hoffman, Hayes concluded, "So if you approach a personality with periodic meetings explaining what's acceptable and what isn't and why, then giving warnings is unnecessary. You're not dealing with a child here, after all."

Child or not, Stern, who felt neglected and abused by management, responded with the deliberate rebelliousness of a juvenile delinquent. In *Private Parts* Stern recalls, "I was pretty out of control but I didn't care. I just wanted to do great radio. I've always felt you can't back down after a certain point."

Stern advanced with a vengeance, setting his sights on the genial Sales. Shortly after coming to WNBC, Sales often remained in the studio after his 10 A.M.-to-3 P.M. shift

to banter with Stern. These innocuous interchanges gradually deteriorated to name-calling. Stern tagged Sales as "old and tired." Since Sales had received management's blessings, Stern retaliated with his own imprecations. Even after Sales retreated from the fray, the war continued.

Hayes may have envisioned a WNBC team, but the Imus/Sales/Stern/Wolfman Jack lineup was nothing more than an disjointed assemblage of oddball personalities. A legendary conflict between Stern and Sales involved the spillage of salad dressing on the studio floor. Fed up with the food remains and garbage Sales and his crew left in the studio, Stern decided to go public with his frustration. During his show, Stern contacted Sales by telephone and declared that if Sales, or one of his staff, did not clean up the mess posthaste Stern would begin to cut the wires of his

"*In personality radio, Don Imus discovered the Mississippi River. Then Howard Stern went off looking for Mars.*"
—Kevin Metheny, a. k. a. "Pig Virus"

Generally Fred Norris enhances the radio show with recorded sound effects, but in this scene from *Private Parts*, Stern improvises some live mouth noises into the microphone for the pleasure of his listening audience.

beloved piano. When Sales and company failed to respond to the threat, Stern broadcast the sound of piano wires being snapped by a wire cutter.

Stern claims this effectively ended his communication with Sales; however, Colford maintains the entire event was a charade and that Stern simply used sound effects to simulate the destruction. Whatever the case, Stern displayed a cunning sense of compelling radio. Listeners could not help but be alternately appalled and amused as they listened to what appeared to be petty infighting gone hideously out of control. Stern's audience tuned in just to hear what would happen next and to see how far the rambunctious jock would go. Unbeknownst to Stern, he was rapidly approaching the outer limits of what management would allow.

# Radio Activity

**In 1901, Italian engineer and inventor Guglielmo Marconi made history when he successfully transmitted a transatlantic long-wave radio signal. The content of this message, which heralded the dawn of the radio age, was the letter S in Morse code. Surely, students of semiology marvel that the original radio broadcast signified the first letter of Stern, Shock Jock, and sexually explicit material.**

**Throughout the twentieth century, various pundits, from statesmen to cartoon characters, have commented on this medium, a child of the electronic age whose growth was stunted due to neglect and a steady diet of pabulum and poison. The following represents a cross section of the crosstalk.**

•"Radio will serve to make the concept of 'Peace on Earth, Good Will Toward Man' a reality."
—James Harbord, former president of Radio Corporation of America

•"Radio could not survive because it was a by-product of advertising. Ability, merit and talent were not requirements of writers and actors working in the industry. Audiences had to be attracted, for advertising purposes, at any cost and by any artifice.... When television belatedly found its way into the home, after stopping off too long at the tavern, the advertisers knew they had a more potent force available for their selling purposes. Radio was abandoned like the bones at a barbecue."
—Fred Allen, *Treadmill to Oblivion*, 1954

•"Country music sucks. All it does is take precious airspace away from shock DJs, whose cruelty and profanity amuse us all."
—Bart Simpson

•"Radio is in the hands of such a lot of fools, trying to anaesthetize the way that you feel."
—Elvis Costello, "Radio, Radio"

•"No matter how good you are in radio, you will always be a scumbag for being a radio personality."
—Howard Stern in *Playboy*

*"I found Howard very amusing on the radio when I wasn't responsible for what he did."* —Kevin Metheny,

The man, the mike, the madness.

## Controlling Interests

In an interview conducted in August 1984 regarding how long he thought WNBC would endure his antics, Stern proclaimed, "Are you kidding? They'll tolerate me until the ratings go down." By the middle of 1985, Stern's ratings were his highest at WNBC, drawing a larger audience share for his program than the entire station in any other time slot. Stern easily outperformed his nemesis, Imus, whose ratings continued to drop. Stern's hubris increased in direct correlation to his skyrocketing ratings. He was

fully aware that his popularity translated into profits for the radio station. Stern was number one, but the executives at WNBC were growing weary of his doing a number on them. In particular, Stern mercilessly excoriated Hayes on the air, calling him "idiot" and "scum." Stern recalls, with great relish, bursting into the Incubus' inner sanctum and nearly coming to blows with the outraged general manager. Stern maintained that the intrusion was part of the boundless comedy of his show, but it was apparent that Hayes felt violated and was not willing to participate in the bit.

Never one to backpedal, Stern proceeded to repeatedly run over Hayes with a viciously comic piece in which "fans" who offered to physically abuse the general manager were countered by a sober Stern who called only for Hayes' ouster. Stern began to believe that he was untouchable, unstoppable, invincible. No longer content to just push the envelope, Stern began to tear it open.

Hate mail and angry phone calls about Stern were nothing new. In Stern's first two years in the Big Apple, the Anti-Defamation League of B'nai Brith's New York City regional office received "more complaints about Howard Stern than about any other single individual or incident in years." WNBC responded to the ADL's complaints by commenting that Stern was a satirist who did not endorse bigotry. Meanwhile, the Federal Communications Commission's Complaints and Investigations Branch of the Enforcement Division was quite familiar with Stern's detractors; Stern had the dubious honor to be one of the few New York radio personalities about whom the FCC received complaints. Regarding these complaints about Stern, Parsons commented, "People will think Howard is hilarious until he says something that affects them. Then they think he's not so funny anymore. I know it's all an act, but some people don't." Such apologies and explanations generally quelled the flames of the average smoldering complainant, but this fire was about to get out of control due to an untimely response to a letter by a Randolph, New Jersey, radio listener.

When he had received no response, the New Jersey man dashed off another note accusing WNBC of being unresponsive and not caring about its listeners' opinions. Rukeyser promptly telephoned the listener and concluded that there was value in his concerns about the content of Stern's show. Tinker was alerted.

"Let somebody else put that shit on the air. It just shouldn't be us."
—Grant Tinker

Stern claims, "When I hear Robin's laugh, I feel that I'm on target." Here Stern hits the bull's-eye.

*"Howard wrote his own epitaph at NBC. The firing was inevitable. He was doing stuff that just wasn't good radio."*

—Bob Sherman

## Statuary Offense

The objectionable content, detailed in the first letter, involved Stern's questioning what the millions of dollars being raised by Chrysler chairman Lee Iacocca to renovate the Statue of Liberty would really be used for. Stern conjectured that perhaps Lady Liberty was to be fit with a bronze tampon or that fifty thousand gallons of copper would be dispensed for her statuesque douching needs.

Following the discussion of New York Harbor's gynocolossus, Stern launched into his favorite obsession (incidentally the subtitle of the first chapter of *Private*

Clad in a groovy shirt, Stern gives the camera a soulful look in a scene from *Private Parts*.

*Parts*): lesbians, lesbians, lesbians. Sapphic lovemaking skills were addressed freely. Evidently, the New Jersey letter writer, who was traveling by car with his children during the unacceptable broadcast, remained tuned in long

enough to gather ammunition against Stern. Rukeyser characterized the grumbling correspondent as "sensible," but one questions the sense of the shocked listener continuing to expose his children to the offending segments—Stern forbids his own children to listen to his show! WNBC's top executives began machinations to remove their top disc jockey from the airwaves. Stern was unaware of these high-level, backroom, underhanded negotiations.

On the air, Stern continued to push the boundaries. One of cohort Norris' bizarre suggestions led to the announcement of the ultimate Dial-a-Date, guaranteed to be abominated by humans, God, and WNBC management—Bestiality Dial-a-Date. Around this time, Stern's old friend Bongarten was informed by his superior, Bob Walsh (whom Tinker describes as a "solid citizen" in his autobiography, *Tinker in Television*), of plans to eighty-six Stern from his perch at 66. Bongarten admonished Stern to lay off the strong material for his own good. Stern professes to have not known, or refused to acknowledge, the import of "or else" implicit in Bongarten's warning. Nonetheless, Stern had the presence of mind to cancel Bestiality Dial-a-Date.

Upstairs at WNBC, Tinker was advised that Stern represented "the difference between profit and loss at the station." The high-minded chairman ordained, "If that's the only way to make money, we shouldn't be in business. Let's get rid of him as fast as we can." Bongarten merely forestalled the inevitable. Attempts to plead a case supporting WNBC's afternoon pariah with Tinker were denied, and Walsh directed Bongarten to fire Stern. Friday, September 27, 1985, was the scheduled day of termination, but WNBC executives were forced to postpone the dismissal until after the weekend as Hurricane Gloria was threatening to wreak havoc across the metropolitan area.

New Yorkers prepared for a devastating storm. Masking-tape Xs were applied to windows to protect against large pieces of flying glass when the deadly gusts arrived. Workers stayed home and commerce came to a veritable standstill in Manhattan, where most businesses remained closed. When the storm finally blew over, around midday, the streets were so devoid of traffic that a pedestrian could walk down the middle of Fifth Avenue encountering only the occasional vehicle. Long Island, where Stern lived, received the brunt of Gloria's torrential rain and wind, but Stern and his crew made it to work. Things got out of control pretty quickly.

The powers that be wanted Stern fired on a Friday so that local media coverage of the event would be dead by Monday. Stern was supposed to have been handed his walking papers when he arrived at work, but neither Bongarten nor Hayes was there to carry out the deed. Stern's final broadcast at WNBC took a vicious turn when Stern was informed that Soupy Sales was about to be syndicated nationally over the NBC Radio Network; Stern had been promised syndication for years. The affront was untenable. Stern went ballistic and threatened to quit WNBC if the rumors were true. Having spewed vitriol for the duration of his show, a sour Stern returned home to windswept, debris-ridden Long Island.

On Monday morning Stern arrived to work on crutches; he had injured himself jogging over the weekend. With more than two hours to showtime, Stern was greeted by Hayes, who sent the hobbled disc jockey by elevator to the sixth floor for a private meeting with Bongarten. While Bongarten calmly terminated Stern, four stories below, Hayes discharged Quivers. Although *The Howard Stern Show* was finished at WNBC, writers Norris and Rosenberg and producer Dell'Abate remained at the station until a replacement DJ was found.

Stern had joined the ranks of the unemployed. There appeared to be no immediate prospects but Stern's agent, Don Buchwald, was upbeat. Buchwald assured Stern that he would be back on the air in New York very soon earning a better salary. The momentarily defeated Stern would return to radio with a single-minded intent: to rule the airwaves and destroy those who would keep him down. Shortly, all pretenders to the throne would bow before the future King of All Media.

*"I'm just a humorist. I'm not anti-anybody."*

First Amendment advocate Stern rallies to support the Texas librarian who lost her job for ordering his first book.

"You cannot go wrong with lesbians. You know I'm not the only one who knows this. I'm just blunt about it."

# CHAPTER FOUR

# Into the Enemy's Camp

"*I will never have a lot of self-esteem. I don't feel very good about myself. I don't think I'm an attractive man, number one. And looks play an important part in how I feel about myself.*"

The fallout following Stern's sudden departure from New York radio was greater than the executives at WNBC had anticipated. Hurricane Gloria was not as devastating as it had promised to be and left the press free to cover more entertaining tempests. All the major local papers reported on Stern's termination.

When asked for comment on the firing, Bongarten offered a prepared statement: "The show has been canceled due to conceptual differences between Howard and the station's manager. He is still under contract with us, but it's unlikely we will put him back on the air." Hayes recorded a similar message, which was broadcast intermittently throughout the afternoon drive-time slot that Stern had previously occupied. Listeners were invited to write in with their opinions regarding the cancellation.

WNBC's solicitousness toward its listeners posed an unexpectedly enormous logistical problem. A deluge of correspondence was directed to Hayes and the switchboard was swamped with telephone calls. Most of the letters (70 percent, according to Hayes) were from supportive Stern fans protesting the cancellation of the show. Additional staff was required to handle the mother lode of mail. WNBC's executives went into overdrive performing damage control. After all, an extremely popular radio personality had been silenced—the station fought to save face and keep listeners.

If WNBC management believed their phrase "conceptual differences" suggested to the public the decision to end the relationship between the station and Stern was mutual, nobody was buying. *The New York Times* wryly covered Stern's dismissal in the "Going Out Guide" and typographically emphasized the suspect phrase with quotation marks. In the meantime, Stern addressed the local media. He claimed to have been given no reason for his dismissal. In interviews, Stern assumed the role of victim, professed to having been blindsided by the firing, and intimated that perhaps a reconciliation could be worked out. Stern proclaimed, "I think I was easy to work with." But there was no going back.

With nowhere to go, Stern weighed his options. WNBC was still bound in a contract with their former afternoon man for another two years. (Stern's salary is estimated to have been around $400,000 a year). The unemployed radio man could have chosen to just sit back and collect a nice paycheck, but Stern wisely decided to keep his name and fame in circulation.

Television beckoned, and on October 22, 1985, Stern made an outrageous appearance on Bill Boggs' short-lived *Comedy Tonight*. Having just returned from a shopping spree at the Pleasure Chest, Stern bound Boggs in a series of leather restraints and cuffs. Silencing Boggs with an S&M mask and gag, Stern seized control of the program returning from the commercial break to announce, "Welcome back to 'The Howard Stern Show.'" A good-natured Boggs went along with the comic bondage and lack of discipline and even put up with being spritzed with seltzer. Stern offered Boggs the backhanded compliment, "Letterman is funnier than you, but he won't let ya do anything to him—which is why you're cool, Bill."

Following this manic television appearance, Stern hooked up with Quivers for theater dates at the Candlewood Playhouse in New Fairfield, Connecticut, and at the Club Bené in Sayreville, New Jersey. At these shows Stern offered paying audiences an uncensored, uninhibited version of his radio show. This was Stern's first real opportunity to come face-to-face with his New York listeners, who

**Previous page (inset):** Looking very Hollywood, the King of All Media dons dark shades and a tux. **Right:** Stern and Quivers at FX Television studios in New York City.

apparently represented a wider demographic than T-shirt-wearing young men and raincoat-clad perverts. Among the attendees were upscale couples and businessmen who responded favorably to Stern's live act. These live performances neatly coincided with Stern's triumphant return to radio.

Don Buchwald, who had arrived with champagne on that fateful final day of September when Stern was fired in an attempt to make light of the situation, now had good reason to celebrate. Buchwald had negotiated what he referred to as a "monumental" deal that would have Stern back on the airwaves on November 18. Refusing to discuss details with the inquisitive press, Buchwald declared, "I can only say Howard will have one of the two best deals on New York radio." WNBC released Stern from his contract. Bob Walsh, the executive who "predicted that Stern would go right across the street to some competing station and get the same kind of numbers against" WNBC, could not have guessed Stern's bankability. Buchwald made certain that Stern's new employers recognized the financial advantages of the arrangement.

## FM—No Static at All

In the topsy-turvy world of radio broadcasting, it is not unusual for a radio station to change hands and formats as quickly as a bored listener can turn the dial. Stern's new radio home was no exception. In less than a decade the station had gone from soft rock to disco to Top 40 as WKTU. Under Infinity Broadcasting's ownership, WKTU's call letters were dropped in favor of WXRK (K-Rock) in the summer of 1985, and the station changed its format to album rock.

Infinity's executive vice president, Mel Karmazin, was looking for a powerful radio personality to take over the afternoon drive slot, one who could draw listeners from the coveted eighteen- to thirty-four-year-old male demographic. Stern was just the man for the job. As an additional incentive, Buchwald provided Karmazin with documentary evidence of a large number of past loyal sponsors who were interested in advertising with Stern again. An impressed Karmazin signed on the dotted line, and Stern was brought aboard as the highest paid (speculations suggest $500,000 for the first year) personality at WXRK. His mind was still in the gutter, but things were looking up for Stern.

At a November 6 press conference held at the Beanstalk Restaurant (ironically the WNBC sponsor whose lunch for Soupy Sales' show had led to the piano wire–cutting incident), K-Rock announced that Stern would command the 2 to 6 P.M. time slot. His new employers were fully aware of what they were getting with Stern. K-Rock's vice president and general manager, Tom Chiusano, stated definitively that Stern could do whatever he wanted. Management vowed to provide the great radio artist with unrestrained creative license. Stern took stage and swore to a rollickingly unique, orgiastic return to New York radio. Having pronounced AM radio dead on his arrival to FM, Stern publicly embraced K-Rock's music and format. If WNBC represented the dark ages, K-Rock marked Stern's radio renaissance.

Hiring a disc jockey who had a history of deriding playlists must have seemed an odd choice for K-Rock, which was fiercely courting the rock and roll demographic. However, Stern was willing to play along and play the records. Mixing music into his show was a small concession considering the absolute freedom he was promised. He had the full support of management and was given back his radio family. Having signed on Quivers, K-Rock brought Norris and Rosenberg over from WNBC to join the cast. Shortly after Stern's debut, producer Dell'Abate, who still lingered

A longstanding relationship that's had its ups and downs, the interplay between Stern and Quivers is crucial to *The Howard Stern Show*.

# Kicking the Sidekick

As producer, Gary Dell'Abate probably has the most thankless task in the Stern organization. Harking back to his early days at WNBC, Stern has made a practice of mocking, chastising, and generally humiliating his producers. Dell'Abate's predecessor was Lee Davis, whom Stern required to make embarrassing retail purchases, such as feminine hygiene products, gay pornography, and hemorrhoid salves—while carrying a tape recorder. To further degrade his producers, Stern preceded their Christian names with "Boy." "Boy Lee" defected to produce Soupy Sales' show and eventually went on to become a successful general manager at another radio station. "Boy Gary" took over the position at $150 per week.

For more than a decade, Dell'Abate has received a lion's share of grief and abuse. Under attack have been Dell'Abate's teeth (described by Stern as "unevenly colored tombstone-size caps"), intellect (Stern once called the Association for Retarded Citizens to get Dell'Abate tested), and olfaction (a lost bet required the producer to press his nose to a flatulent Stern's buttocks). All this for a man whom Stern acknowledges does his extensively backbreaking dirty work. The explanation (not an excuse): pitiless abuse makes for good radio.

Aside from playing Stern's acquiescent whipping boy, Dell'Abate is also inadvertently responsible for what has become perhaps the most famous phrase to move beyond the confines of Stern's show and into the mass consciousness of pop culture: "Baba Booey." The genesis of the nickname follows: a collector of cartoon cels, Dell'Abate said on the air that he was in the market for a artwork depicting Quick Draw McGraw's sidekick, Baba Looey. He mispronounced the character's name as Baba Booey. Stern, who thought the whole concept idiotic to begin with, proceeded to mock the ill-informed collector (who didn't even know the correct name of his "favorite" character) ceaselessly. From that point forward Dell'Abate was dubbed Baba Booey.

Variations on the theme exist (Fa Fa Flooley, Ma Ma Monkey, and Sa Sa Smelly to name but a few), but "Baba Booey" has achieved a special place in the multimedia soundscape. Stern's fans in particular enjoy telephoning television and radio personalities during live broadcasts only to explode into the anarchic non sequitur, "Baba Booey. Stern rules."

at NBC's rapidly sinking flagship station, was rescued at Stern's request and pulled aboard at K-Rock. Stern and his gang were ready to give New York an earful.

## "It's a Love Affair"

A couple of years before joining K-Rock, Stern commented, "All radio station managements are the same—they're whores and slobs. The day I don't have ratings is the day I can kiss my ass good-bye." Stern stepped into his new position at K-Rock with a secure foothold in the ratings and immediately began to climb. On the way down was K-Rock's morning man, Jay Thomas. Thomas, another of Buchwald's clients, made $260,000 a year, but after four years he had failed to provide the station the morning jump-start it needed. Stern's high ratings led to talks about moving the new afternoon drive man to the prime morning slot. It wouldn't take long.

In the first week of January 1986, Thomas was let go. Stern took over the morning show on February 17. It was payback time for the vengeful Stern, now in a position to go

head-to-head with Imus, who remarked, "If Howard Stern beats me, I'll eat a dead dog's penis." Having miscalculated Stern's potential, Imus would soon be forced to eat his words rather than what he'd promised. Stern took K-Rock from twenty-first in the ratings to number one in less than a year. Imus would plummet to twenty-seventh place.

Stern set the tone of his show from the get-go:

STERN: If I could jam my tongue into K-Rock's throat right now I would. [Sloppy kissing noises, the crew responds with vocal disgust, wet sex noises, sound effect: BO-IING!!!]

QUIVERS: It's a love affair.

STERN: Let me tell you something: I love this place.

Stern served up the sonic orgy he had promised New York radio listeners. His audience was regularly titillated with graphic descriptions of in-studio sexual shenanigans. Contrary to the claim that Stern's radio show left nothing to the imagination, it was precisely Stern's appeal to the sexually active imagination of his audience that kept them tuned in. This was an entirely new generation of radio theater. Women stripped for Dial-a-Date segments, shaved their pubic regions, and bent over Stern's knee for on-air spankings. A new level of intimate interactivity was reached when female listeners who had called in were persuaded to straddle their speakers as Stern and company hummed deeply in order to impart orgasmic vibrations for the speaker/phone sex partners.

Stern's rated-X radio excited some, incited others. Playing up his bad boy persona, Stern appeared costumed as the devil, grasping a barbed pitchfork while towering above a tabletop radio, for a *People Weekly* photo shoot. Despite the goofy satanic pose, Stern declares, "I guarantee you what I'm doing is the Lord's work. I am absolutely making people laugh at the most miserable part of their life—that's the morning commute."

With his new position and growing ratings, Stern began to expand his team and K-Rock was all too happy to accommodate their revolutionary new morning man. Initially, Steve Chaconas, one of the original members of the unpaid DC-101 Think Tank, was hired to augment the writing staff. The arrangement, which demanded the Washington-based Chaconas to commute to New York, was less than satisfactory and the new writer was soon let go. Filling the void was longtime contributor Jackie "the Joke Man" Martling, who was finally brought on as a full-time employee.

Stern, Quivers, Norris, Martling, and Dell'Abate comprised the nucleus of the atomic radio device known as *The Howard Stern Show*. Their effect on local and national radio would be explosive.

## Out of the Shadows

At K-Rock, Stern was able to overcome a problem that had plagued him for years. A requisite element of the broadcast was the traffic report, a boring feature that Stern felt impeded the smooth flow of his comedy. As part of his K-Rock broadcast, Stern rudely interrupted and lewdly interjected during Shadow Traffic correspondent Susan Berkowitz's report. Berkowitz, renamed "Beserkowitz," made valiant efforts to describe traffic conditions over Stern's excessively puerile verbiage. In the same manner that he personalized commercial spots to mesh with his comic onslaught, Stern

turned the traffic reports into inquisitions of Berkowitz's sex life that were liberally sprinkled with insults.

The strained interaction between Stern and the traffic reporter, who gamely hung in there, made for fascinating

Stern has good reason for the broad smile. His success at K-Rock acted as the springboard to widespread syndication and international fame.

*"A lot of what drives me is hate."*

Jackie "the Joke Man" Martling smirks as Stern controls the microphone at KLSX—Stern's Los Angeles radio outlet where he promised to beat the competition "worse than the L.A. police beat Rodney King."

radio. Regular listeners became familiar with the tense interplay and looked forward to those times when Stern's comic excursions bordered on personal trespass. Although Berkowitz was often sorely tested, it became fairly obvious that she willingly participated in an exchange that was merely part of the act. After all, in the realm of the radio talk show, "good" is not measured by virtue, but by ratings. Sometimes, listening to Stern's show is like eavesdropping on a conversation by pressing a drinking glass against the wall to hear the neighbors' bickering—irresistibly compelling but sometimes embarrassingly wrong. Berkowitz, who changed her last name to Berkley, left Shadow Traffic in 1987 to start her own school of broadcasting.

## Revenge Is Bitter

On May 5, 1986, rather than celebrate the coming of spring by dancing around a maypole, Stern summoned a horde of thousands to celebrate the death of his former employer, WNBC. This event marked the first of many "funerals" that would be conducted by Stern, who was no longer content to just beat his competitors in the ratings; he needed to bury them.

Stern was in good shape, having tripled K-Rock's morning audience, and WNBC, having retained only 20 percent of its former afternoon listeners, was going down the tubes. Stern wanted to rub his victory in Imus' "alligator-face." In *Miss America*, Stern traces his need to utterly destroy the enemy to a miserable youth spent as every bully's punching bag. To Stern's mind, Imus had greater significance than merely being WNBC's competing morning man. Imus represented "Fat Johnny," the neighborhood bully who brutalized Stern in his geeky youth.

Regarding Stern's vengeful nature, Quivers told David Remnick in *The New Yorker*: "Revenge is not sweet enough, though. Howard is constantly revisiting the past, and somehow it isn't enough to have the entire world be in love with you. He still wants the people who didn't love him before to love him now." In his trademark straightforward way, Stern puts it more succinctly: "Either you're on my side or you're dead."

The NBC funeral was relatively slapdash and lacked the excessive coverage and hype that would become the earmark of future publicity stunts devised by Stern. Well aware of the potential headaches in gathering proper permits to conduct a rally in midtown Manhattan, Stern sidestepped the bureaucratic issue entirely. With minimal preparation and zero fanfare, Stern asked his listeners to join him, after he signed off, in front of the Beanstalk Restaurant—

## Bully for you!

In addition to WNBC, other local radio stations were suffering because of Stern's success. The immense popularity of his show set the stage for syndication into other radio markets. Stern claims his bloodthirsty attacks against Imus were in large part due to the veteran radio man taking credit for an act he had stolen from Stern. Indeed, Stern's novel approach to morning radio begot a spate of pale imitators. With syndication, Stern used the opportunity to broadcast in new cities as a declaration of war against the competing morning jocks, many of whom were also ripping him off. As part of the ongoing shtick, every dip in the competitors' ratings was reported by Stern as if the Stern army had wiped out another enemy battalion. Stern would not relent until the humiliated enemy lay bloody in the trenches, losing life and ratings.

Particularly gratifying for Stern was the ultimate demise of WNBC. The station that turned a profit while Stern was aboard took a serious financial drubbing following his exit. NBC cut their losses and sold off the quickly diminishing asset that, once upon a time, was the gem of their national radio network. In the fall of 1988, WNBC was replaced by WFAN, an all-sports station that retained Imus' services as the morning man.

An irony suited to the nasty world of radio rivalry would come back to haunt Stern. Infinity Broadcasting purchased WFAN from Emmis Broadcasting Corporation, essentially making Stern and Imus coworkers. Imus was reported to have been making $2.5 million a year—no doubt a sore spot for the fiercely competitive Stern. Before long, more blood would flow as Stern slashed his way into the national radio market.

*"I still think I'm garbage and that's the healthiest thing about me."*

an advantageous location as the Stern sponsor was practically downstairs from the NBC offices. A surprisingly large mob awaited Stern who, wearing a hooded black robe befitting the grim reaper, arrived in an open limousine with Robin Quivers, portraying Death's bride, dressed in white with a black veil.

The guerrilla nature of Stern's spontaneous street theater required that the mock funeral ceremony be quick and to the point—concluded before New York's Finest stepped in to disband the increasingly unruly rabble. Addressing the throng over a public address system, Stern played the Angel of Death and wished the Ten Plagues upon NBC. With the pronouncement of each plague Stern's acolytes added vociferous assent. However, after "locusts, boils, and low ratings," seven plagues shy, Stern bid a not-so-fond farewell to NBC and made a speedy exodus from the police. As the conquering hero departed, he had one last gesture for his former employers—a raised middle finger.

## At Home and Abroad

The year 1986 was turning out to be a banner year for Stern and his families. On May 8, Stern's second daughter, Debra, was born. The Stern radio family was expecting its own joyous event. Talks were underway to syndicate *The Howard Stern Show* outside the New York market. Infinity Broadcasting's rock and roll radio outlet in Philadelphia, WYSP, was foundering in the ratings. WYSP's program director, Andy Bloom, strategized that a simulcast of Stern's New York show in the City of Brotherly Love would give the station a requisite shot in the arm and provide the competition a well-deserved kick in the ass. Stern was intrigued.

The common belief was that Stern's show was too invested in a New York sensibility to play to an out-of-town audience. Critics believed the seventy-eight miles between the two major cities represented an unbridgeable gap for a morning radio personality. Generally, the innocuous or

*"I'm not proud of the fact that I am driven like an idiot to beat other radio guys into the ground. But I'm honest about it."*

# The Self-Hurt Section

**For all of Stern's vicious attacks on his "enemies," there is no one whom he disparages more than himself. Inverting the basic tenets defined by the self-help psychology gurus, Stern has spawned a perpetual regimen of self-hurt that could be summed up in one T-shirt-worthy proverb: "In order to truly hate someone you must first learn to hate yourself." At the diseased heart of Stern's self-flagellation is the precept that comedy is born of suffering. Rather than lose his comic edge, Stern hones it daily on the whetstone of self-deprecation.**

**A Freudian explanation of his neuroses might reveal that Stern suffers a form of penis envy—he wishes his was larger. Stern has turned this supposed shortcoming into a source of comic material to which he returns frequently. He has described himself as being hung like a pimple, an acorn, a raisin—among other diminutive similes. However in a *Playboy* interview, Stern revealed that fully erect he is "at least average, five to six inches....Flaccid, I'm in a sorry state."**

**In the following quotations Stern explores his ongoing love-hate relationship with himself:**

"I will never have a lot of self-esteem. I don't feel very good about myself. I don't think I'm an attractive man, number one. And looks play an important part in how I feel about myself."

"I look like Big Bird on acid."

"I'm not the healthiest person in the world."

"I'm not proud of the fact that I am driven like an idiot to beat other radio guys into the ground. But I'm honest about it."

**In *Miss America*, Stern's sad concession "I suck at almost everything" is balanced with a definitive statement of self-worth: "I'm the best" at radio. Stern, the self-hating narcissist, doesn't mince words: "No one else has a right to be on the radio but me."**

**All hail the conquering zero.**

generic has a better chance of translating from one market to another. Stern was out to prove all the naysayers wrong. Success in such intermarket maneuvering was unprecedented. Then again, Philadelphia had never been exposed to anything like Stern.

WYSP's rival station, WMMR (once considered the nation's finest progressive rock station), had a lock on the morning time slot. The prefab "Morning Zoo" format ruled the day, with Zoo Keeper John DeBella pulling in a massive 13 ratings share. (The Morning Zoo is often attributed to have originated with disc jockey Scott Shannon—the competitor upon whom Stern wished cancer shortly after going on the air at K-Rock.)

DeBella had a good thing going, earning at least $1 million the year he was number one in Philly—presumably due to the lack of any real competition. Upon learning that Stern was to challenge him in the local market, DeBella insisted, "Stern thinks I'll shake and quake in my boots, but I don't lose." In subsequent interviews, DeBella asserted the superiority of his "show" over Stern's "act" and maintained that he would prevail as Philadelphia's reigning morning man.

Prior to his August 18, 1986, debut on WYSP, Stern had sized up DeBella as the latest manifestation of his personal bugaboo: the neighborhood bully. Stern became familiar with rumors of DeBella's pomposity. Evidently, it was not enough for DeBella to behave as Philly's supreme radio being; he required lesser creatures to grovel in his presence. Gary Dell'Abate would frequently recall the misfortune of having interned under DeBella years earlier. An arrogant taskmaster, DeBella would not allow his interns to make eye contact with him or speak directly to him. In Stern's mind, DeBella had replaced Imus as an opponent that needed to be thoroughly ruined.

There was a manipulative method to Stern's madness. Stern discovered that the more personal he made his show, the better the response. It was not enough to pursue a ratings victory; the average listener couldn't care less about ratings. However, a good blood-and-guts battle with an identifiable opponent pulled in listeners. Stern, the great radio war strategist, knew what to do to win over the Philadelphia audience: he would need to demonize, demoralize, and destroy DeBella.

**Opposite:** Stern strikes a dramatically thoughtful pose.

"I may be a lot of things.
I may even be what the
FCC thinks. But an idiot
I'm not."

# CHAPTER FIVE

# The Medium Is the Sensual Massage

**Previous page (inset):** Stern at a book signing for Robin Quivers' autobiography at FX Television studios. **Below:** The King of All Media is joined on stage by Jessica Hahn dressed (barely) in one of her crowd-pleasing, eye-catching, sexual-fantasy-provoking outfits during one of Stern's infamous "funerals."

Stern greeted his Philadelphia listeners on August 18, 1986, with the foreboding salutation "Welcome to your worst nightmare." In truth, DeBella did most of the tossing and turning. Stern had worked himself up and had compiled an arsenal of insults. To achieve victory in the alien radio market, Stern set out to identify what he perceived to be DeBella's weak spots and then relentlessly hammered away. The assaults focused on DeBella's appearance (bald with a "walrus" mustache) and personality ("arrogant" and "smug"). Stern projected that not only would he defeat the Zoo Keeper, but that DeBella's wife would leave him and that "Baldy" would ultimately cringe at the feet of King Stern, begging to be allowed to return to radio. Like a psychotic prophet of doom, Stern launched a gruesome unholy war in the name of good radio. The results he got were surprising, as all his predictions started to come true.

Stern manipulated his Philadelphia listeners brilliantly. Unlike other disc jockeys who were required by their stations to appear at arbitrary promotional events, Stern masterminded his own self-promotional events. He promised Philadelphia a festive funeral fete as soon as he surpassed the Zoo Keeper. DeBella had a massive ratings lead and probably felt secure enough to ignore Stern rather than fight back. During a televised interview, a self-satisfied DeBella declared that he was unbeatable and concluded, "I'm that damn good." Stern took umbrage at the dismissive and disdainful DeBella, and was inspired anew to demolish the enemy. Regarding Stern's bloodthirstiness, Philadelphia journalist Joe Logan commented, "[Stern] told me, on occasion, that DeBella, at the time, represented to him every bully who had ever pushed him around, every cool kid who made fun of him. John DeBella became the embodiment of what he had to crush to get where he wanted to get."

Having established himself as a recognizable voice on the Philadelphia airwaves, Stern plotted his next offensive. In a twisted variation on a theme, Stern demonstrated that it is better to give than receive and telephoned DeBella while both men were in the middle of their morning broadcasts. DeBella answered all calls to the Morning Zoo hotline with "Yazoo!" When Stern identified himself, DeBella instantly hung up the telephone. During one such call, an employee at WMMR decided to punish Stern and put him on hold. Since WMMR plays its broadcast signal for callers put on hold, Stern was richly rewarded with a direct feed of DeBella's show. Prior to this moment, Stern had been limited to attacking the Morning Zoo in general, but now he had the unique opportunity to remorselessly trash DeBella and company in real time.

Stern's efforts to contact DeBella by telephone inspired one peculiarly monomaniacal listener to join the ranks of the cranks. Tom Cipriano, a shipping clerk from Philadelphia, assumed the nom de guerre Captain Janks and applied himself to calling into WMMR to mock DeBella on the air. "I just called to say I loathe you" could well have served as Cipriano's slogan. Cipriano recorded the exchanges and sent them off to Stern. As Stern branched out into more markets, other phony phone callers would volunteer their disservices, but Captain Janks would forever be known as "the king of all cranks."

On May 10, 1990, having finally seized the number one spot over DeBella, Stern brought his entourage to Philadelphia. In contrast to the Imus funeral, DeBella's burial was preceded by planning and much fanfare. Stern would not let this victory go without proper media coverage, so he wisely stayed on the air throughout the entire procession.

Following a press conference that featured Scott Salem (the radio show's engineer) dressed to look like DeBella laying in a coffin, Stern conducted the Zoo Keeper's funeral from a stage in Rittenhouse Square—shouting distance from WMMR's studios. Robed in liturgical vestments and crowned with a miter, Stern conducted the funeral rites and rallied the "mourners" into a frenzy—an appearance by a nearly naked Jessica Hahn helped to increase the crowd's fervor. Stern, the reigning king of Philadelphia radio, left the stage while the celebration was still at a fever pitch.

Unfortunately for DeBella, all of Stern's gloomy predictions came to pass. Subsequent to his defeat, the Zoo Keeper lost his radio show (September 30, 1993) and his wife (Annette DeBella died in the midst of their bitter divorce), and as a final insult, Stern realized his third prediction by demanding that DeBella come on-air and apologize in order to be allowed to return to radio. Oddly enough, by 1994, Infinity offered to hire the former Zoo Keeper for the afternoon drive slot on their Philadelphia station—but only

## Cranking Up

**Thomas Cipriano's obsessive devotion to abruptly advertise his idol during phone-in segments of national radio and television programs has earned him a branch on Stern's gnarly radio family tree. Apart from his ornate and inventive phony phone calls, Cipriano's association with Stern's show is bizarrely interwoven with the unseemly slaughter of the Zoo Keeper.**

**Cipriano declared war with DeBella after having been slighted by "Baldy" at a public appearance. Cipriano borrowed the name of his commanding officer from his U.S. Army days, Captain Janks, and mobilized a full-scale invasion. Janks lured DeBella into inane exchanges and then bellowed "You suck!" or "Howard rules!" DeBella fought to maintain composure before hanging up.**

**As DeBella's show fell apart (taking a major ratings dive) and his marriage went to pieces, Janks gained the upper hand with the help of Stern. Annette DeBella, the Zoo Keeper's estranged wife who was in dire financial straits (DeBella had allegedly canceled her credit cards), agreed to go on the Stern show and participate in a Dial-a-Date segment, for which she was compensated $5,000. The lucky bachelor she selected was none other than the thorn in her husband's side, Captain Janks. The unlikely couple's date is chronicled on Stern's *Butt Bongo Fiesta* video. Annette takes a jab at husband John and allows Janks to kiss and fondle her briefly on camera. But this episode has a devastating coda: Annette DeBella was found dead, presumably by suicide, not long after her date.**

**As for Janks, he has become a legendary phony phone caller, inspiring legions of others to fight their way onto the airwaves. The calls of these minions guarantee Stern's enjoyment of an endless, if unpredictable, source of free publicity. In 1992, the calls received national media attention when a politically impolite caller contacted the *Today* show and asked presidential candidate Ross Perot, "Have you ever had the desire to mind-meld with Howard Stern's penis?" As with all shrewd politicos, Perot proffered no comment.**

HOWARD STERN
THE KING OF ALL MEDIA!

HOWARD STERN RULES

with Stern's approval. Stern magnanimously put his rancor aside and allowed Infinity to employ the vanquished and groveling DeBella. In an interview with *New York Magazine*, Stern remarked, "I try to analyze why I'm so damn vicious, and I realize it's because radio is the only thing I'm good at." For those put off by his cruelty, Stern admits, "It is ugly. It's the ugliest side of me." But he adds paradoxically, "That's what makes my show interesting."

## Watch What You Say

While Stern focused on beating DeBella, a more serious battle was brewing. An elite, powerful force planned to move in on Stern—the Federal Communications Commission was about to assume a stance from which they would not back down. Created in 1934, the FCC is an independent U.S. government agency that oversees all radio, television, wire, and cable transmissions originating in the United States. Appointed by the president, the five-member commission grants radio station licenses, assigns frequencies, and reviews program content. FCC resolves had been instrumental in the advent of FM radio, but suddenly it appeared that the commission was determined to prevent certain types of FM radio.

Complaints about Stern had been directed to the FCC since way back in his Washington days. Having monitored Stern's show for objectionable content, the commission determined that the offending material was more a question of personal taste than obscenity. The FCC rightly concluded

*"The interpretation has been too narrow. We will apply the generic definition and not limit it arbitrarily to seven specific words."*
—Diane Killory, FCC general counsel

that no action against Stern was needed—this was a discretionary issue in the hands of the broadcasters. Philadelphia would change all that.

Accustomed to the insipid blathering of such alleged entertainment as the Morning Zoo, Philadelphians did not know what to make of Stern. Colford reports that in Stern's first three months at WYSP, Philadelphians filed more complaints with the FCC than New Yorkers had in the last three years. However, the statistical significance of this increase is negligible considering that out of half a million Philadelphia listeners, there were only thirty-five complaints. But the "volume" of negative correspondence could not be ignored or easily dismissed. In late November 1986, Infinity Broadcasting was contacted by the FCC and ordered to respond within thirty days to listeners' charges that Stern's broadcast violated Philadelphia's community standards.

Karmazin responded to the FCC and confessed that Stern's controversial and provocative show was "comedic in nature" but sometimes ran the risk of offending those with "delicate sensibilities." Nonetheless, he maintained, Stern's use of sexually oriented language was protected speech. As to the charges that the show could be considered obscene or indecent by local community standards, Karmazin was sure to point out that the most vocal complaint, voiced by the Rev. Donald E. Wildmon (head of the National Federation for Decency, "a Christian organization promoting the biblical ethic of decency in the media"), hailed from Tupelo, Mississippi—not even remotely a Philadelphia suburb. More importantly, Karmazin contended, Stern had not violated what broadcasters looked to as the general FCC guidelines, which had been in place for nearly a decade. The problem was that over time the lines had become blurred. To fully appreciate the magnitude of the FCC's action, see Five Against Seven on the next page.

# Five Against Seven

On October 30, 1973, at 2 P.M., New York's WBAI-FM (owned by the Pacifica Foundation) broadcast comedian George Carlin's "Filthy Words" monologue. Carlin's hysterical twelve-minute exploration of "the words you couldn't say on the public, ah, airwaves, um, the ones you definitely wouldn't say, ever" (from his 1972 album *Class Clown*) was included as part of a program about contemporary society's attitude toward language. According to Supreme Court documentation, "A man, who stated that he had heard the broadcast while driving with his young son, wrote a letter complaining to the Commission. He stated that, although he could perhaps understand the 'record's being sold for private use, I certainly cannot understand the broadcast of same over the air that, supposedly, you control.'"

In response, the FCC issued a declaratory order and held that Pacifica could be subject to administrative sanctions possibly jeopardizing the station's license. The United States Court of Appeals for the District of Columbia Circuit reversed the FCC order after finding it tantamount to censorship. Ultimately, the case was heard before the highest court in the land.

At the heart of the matter was the FCC's definition that the "concept of 'indecent' is intimately connected with the exposure of children to language that describes, in terms patently offensive as measured by contemporary community standards for the broadcast medium, sexual or excretory activities and organs, at times of the day when there is a reasonable risk that children may be in the audience." The U.S. Supreme Court sided with the FCC and on July 3, 1978, overturned the circuit court's reversal. In the Court's majority opinion, Justice Stevens opined:

> "First, the broadcast media have established a uniquely pervasive presence in the lives of all Americans. Patently offensive, indecent material presented over the airwaves confronts the citizen, not only in public, but also in the privacy of the home, where the individual's right to be left alone plainly outweighs the First Amendment rights of an intruder.... Because the broadcast audience is constantly tuning in and out, prior warnings cannot completely protect the listener or viewer from unexpected program content. To say that one may avoid further offense by turning off the radio when he hears indecent language is like saying that the remedy for an assault is to run away after the first blow."

Yes, but one must question the parental paralysis that affects these "unwilling" listeners and prevents them from turning off the radio shortly after the "assault" commences. Perhaps they have been beaten senseless by the verbal blows. Stevens continues: "Second, broadcasting is uniquely accessible to children.... Pacifica's broadcast could have enlarged a child's vocabulary in an instant."

In effect, by upholding the FCC's reprimand, the Supreme Court was not only strangling free speech but limiting its lexicon. First Amendment advocates were horrified. Broadcasters were not happy with the Court's interpretation, or misinterpretation, of the Constitution, but at least they had a rough idea of what was permissible. Carlin's septet of "Filthy Words" became the industry's criteria. For the record, the original "seven dirty words" were: shit, piss, fuck, cunt, cocksucker, motherfucker, and tits. Incidentally, Stern's original contract with Infinity specifically forbade the use of the seven words as well as "douche bag" and "scumbag" (since renegotiating his contract in 1996, Stern has enlarged his on-air vocabulary to include the last two words).

Dormant for almost ten years, the sleeping five-headed beast arose from its slumber. The commission's general counsel, Jack D. Smith, informed the press, "The time of day a program is broadcast, for instance, when children might be listening, is a factor. In addition are standards set in a 1978 Supreme Court case, which the commission won, establishing seven words that cannot be spoken on radio." Smith's statement insinuated that the commission was prepared to go beyond the "seven dirty words" criteria in their examination of Stern.

By law, the FCC was empowered to review programming for indecency but prohibited from acting as a censor; however, their action against Infinity Broadcasting marked the beginning of a clampdown on all broadcasters. The five commissioners, led by chairman Mark Fowler, ushered in a new era of censorship disguised as decency enforcement.

# Narrow Minds and Wide Definitions

Infinity stood by its morning man. Although he was not directed to tone down his act by his employers, Stern appeared to exercise a little more discretion in his on-air diatribes than usual following the FCC's letter. Karmazin summarized his lengthy response to the FCC simply: "Howard Stern is a comedian. He does humor." The FCC was not laughing and found Karmazin's argument invalid.

On April 16, 1987, the commission decided unanimously to adopt measures that would severely limit explicit language regarding sex and bodily functions in the electronic media. This was a major shift in policy for the regulatory agency. The FCC looked to their definition of indecent language as set forth in the Pacifica case and upheld by the Supreme Court as the new rule by which to measure indecency. As proponents of free speech feared, the FCC replaced the specific "seven dirty words" standard with the broader, more ambiguous definition of indecency: "language or material that depicts or describes, in terms patently offensive as measured by contemporary community standards for the broadcast medium, sexual or excretory activities or organs."

Broadcasters were in a bind. The new definition was too broad and lacked specificity. Regarding Stern, FCC general counsel Diane Killory proclaimed, "Some of his material constitutes actionable indecency." Fortunately, the FCC held back from severely penalizing Infinity (two California radio stations, unrelated to Stern's show or Infinity, were also cited for having broadcast "indecent" material at the time) on the grounds that the station might have been unaware of any wrongdoing considering the commission's past enforcement practices. Killory cautioned, "Today, we're warning. Tomorrow (if he continues), we'll impose a more severe sanction—namely a fine."

The future held dark promises of license review, reprimand, and/or revocation. Commenting on the FCC's decision, Karmazin stated, "We took the seven dirty words and we said, 'Don't say these things,' and Howard Stern never said those things. Now if they say 'Now it's 12 dirty words,' Howard will not say those things. If they're saying, 'You can't discuss sex on the radio,' we don't think we'll conform with that. We'll fight that on constitutional grounds."

In the aftermath of the decision, scores of broadcasters contacted the FCC requesting clarification of the commission's vague new obscenity policy. What precisely should be considered "patently offensive"? The FCC either refused, or more likely, was unable to define, their deliberately vague, oppressive edict. Infinity's lawyer, Steven Lerman, elegantly described the difficulty in offering advice on the basis of the commission's nebulous guidelines: "It's like trying to catch a cloud."

On April 21, 1987, Stern spent most of his show discussing the FCC situation. The relentless self-promoter was thrilled to be at the center of a controversy that made for extensive free publicity. Celebrity supporters such as the host of *Lifestyles of the Rich and Famous,* Robin Leach, and head of the Guardian Angels Lisa Sliwa phoned Stern. Ultimately, Stern was frustrated that his fellow broadcasters failed to express their solidarity and rally to his defense. Stern declared to his audience, "I am the last bastion of the First Amendment," and invited them to demonstrate in protest of the FCC decision. Three days later, thousands of

Arms held high, Stern gives the thumbs up to his fans who have paved the road to the palace for the King of All Media.

Stern's fans gathered in Dag Hammarskjöld Plaza outside the United Nations building for the demonstration, which was broadcast live on K-Rock and WYSP.

Wearing his trademark sunglasses and a horizontally striped prisoner's uniform, Stern was joined by performers Leslie West, Phoebe Snow, Richie Havens, and Al Lewis. Stern and Quivers led the assembled crowd in chants such as "Two, four, six, thirty, the FCC is plain dirty." Then Lewis (best known for his role as Grampa on television's *The Munsters*), a regular visitor to Stern's show, addressed the assembled masses, urging them to proclaim their reason for attending the rally. The outspoken Lewis declared their purpose in a rallying cry, quickly taken up by the crowd: "Fuck the FCC!" Without a seven-second delay in place, one of the seven words escaped over the airwaves. Stern wrestled the microphone from Lewis. Luckily, the FCC declined to punish the two stations that inadvertently aired the profanity. Although they were cleared of any wrongdoing regarding the 1986 complaints, Stern and Infinity were essentially put on notice—further scrutiny and sanctions would follow.

**Below:** The infamous April 24, 1987, rally at Dag Hammarskjöld Plaza to protest the FCC's crackdown on "indecency" was broadcast live.

**Opposite:** Protesting the new era of radio censorship, FCC "prisoner" Stern is joined by "Grampa" Al Lewis.

which was going toe-to-toe with the big three networks. Fox's entry in the late-night talk show race, *Late Show Featuring Joan Rivers*, was lagging in the ratings, and rumors abounded that Stern was being seriously considered to replace Rivers as host. Stern himself assumed he had a lock on the position when Joan Rivers (who happens to be one of Stern's friends) was let go in the middle of May. Stern had already completed five pilot episodes for Fox and ceaselessly hyped the imminent broadcast of his television venture during his radio show. Stern could not wait for the pilots to air. His fans could not wait to see their hero conquer a new medium. Wait they would. And wait.

Without explanation, Fox refused to discuss air dates for the pilots. The upstart network's failure to comment on Stern's show did not bode well. News filtered down that the pilots were being screened by test audiences. The focus group screenings (common industry practice when testing a new show) were a slap in the face. An annoyed Stern began to vent his frustration with Fox on the air. Throughout the summer, Stern attacked the Fox executives' intellect and chided their programming as substandard. According to Colford, Fox had decided to shelve the pilots. Fed up with Stern's grousing, the network executives broke their silence in the matter by leaking a negative appraisal of the shows to the press. The prevailing opinion at Fox was that the pilots were "poorly produced, in poor taste" and "boring."

The damaging critical assessment seemed extreme and unfair. Surely Fox's minuscule budget was the reason for the poor production values and they were well aware that Stern was not reputed for his "good taste." Indeed, the episodes bore little evidence of the excitement Stern brought to his radio show—but whose fault was that? From the start, Fox seized creative control. The network restricted Norris' and Martling's input and assigned writers not in sync with Stern to create the show. As a result, Stern was constrained by a typically unimaginative talk show format, the very sort of format he regularly mocked and reviled. Stern retaliated that "the idiots at Fox" did not understand him and suggested that they were "wimps" who had succumb to pressure from the FCC. But the failure of the Fox show had an upside. The lesson learned, according to Stern, was that to do television he would have to do it his way. By taking matters into his own hands, Stern would discover immense creative benefits and financial rewards.

**Above:** Joan Rivers is overwhelmed by aggressive book promoter Stern.

**Opposite:** Stern gives new meaning to "killing the audience" in this sketch from his WWOR television show, which is making fun of a shooting at a Long Island movie theater.

## Out Foxed

In addition to his weekday morning show, Stern had a syndicated weekend radio show, which he described as "a Johnny Carson show for the warped." Available in a limited number of markets, the weekend show, which generally included a visiting celebrity, was canceled in early 1987. This brief foray into syndication was advantageous in that it temporarily placed Stern in the spotlight as a nationally recognized media figure. This recognition opened the door to discussions with the fledgling Fox Broadcasting Network,

## Video Thrilled the Radio Star

Stern rebounded from the Fox disappointment and developed his own pay-per-view cable television special. Touted as a television version of his radio show, Stern promised his fans that he was completely in charge and that the show would not be subject to FCC regulations. Billed as *Howard Stern's Underpants and Negligee Party*, the special aired February 27, 1987, to the approximately sixty thousand cable subscribers in the New York area willing to shell out the $19.95. The show was performed live before a studio audience. In order to be admitted to the event, one was required to strip down to one's Skivvies at Stern's request. The two-and-a-half-hour televised orgy would have made Caligula proud.

The "party" featured numerous guests (celebrities, comedians, and other media oddities) who appeared regularly on the radio show. Following a Lesbian Dial-a-Date segment, Leslie West, former guitarist for the rock group Mountain, performed a solo version of the group's hit "Mississippi Queen." Fred Norris goose-stepped out as Kurt Waldheim, Jr., and conducted a contest of "Guess Who's the Jew" with special guest Jessica Hahn. In a troubling sociological experiment titled "Bum Makeover," Anthony Bartow, a homeless man who was living in the New York City subway, was offered a complete makeover. After repairing to a hotel for a shower and shave, Bartow, dressed in a new suit, was treated to a shopping spree. Festooned with parting gifts such as a mattress from Stern sponsor Dial-a-Mattress, a set of luggage, and various odds and ends, Bartow was returned by limousine to his subway stop. The most unforgettable moment of the evening, however, was when future "Wack Packer" Vincent Mazzeo, with assistance from Quivers, liberally doused his underwear in lighter fluid and attempted to panfry an egg over his flaming groin. Mazzeo, overcome by the intense heat, tore off what remained of his undergarments and proceeded to ignite his bare buttocks. The crowd went wild.

For those who missed it live, the "party" was made available on videotape for $24.95. It was the first of four videotapes to be successfully marketed by Stern through his 800-52-STERN telephone sales number.

## Sore Spot

By late 1989, Stern still lacked a television deal; the taint of the failed Fox fiasco lingered. Rather than wait any longer, Stern produced his second public spectacle for his hungry fans. Advertised as *U.S. Open Sores*, the centerpiece of the festivities was a tennis match between Stern and his producer, Gary Dell'Abate, scheduled for October 7, 1989, at Nassau Coliseum in Uniondale, Long Island. The sixteen-thousand-seat arena sold out in a remarkable four hours.

Jackie "the Joke Man" Martling warmed up the Coliseum crowd with a fifteen-minute set of his nonstop assortment of gags. Next, the national anthem was performed on a portable Casio keyboard by Celestine, a paraplegic woman who played with her tongue. The first match of the evening featured Robin Quivers against foot fetishist and Stern show regular, Darren. Quivers' easy victory released her from the undesired attentions of Darren "the Footlicker," who was banned from Stern's show and forbidden to contact Quivers ever again.

The much ballyhooed grudge match between Stern and Dell'Abate was a rout, with the producer easily defeating the popular morning man. Stern's mood soured following his humiliating defeat. After insulting "Boy Gary," Stern turned on "Grampa" Al Lewis, who offered commentary during the match. Stern announced that the current television remake *The Munsters Today* was superior to the original *The Munsters*. The audience booed noisily at Stern the poor sport.

Underwear burner Mazzeo demonstrated new pyrotechnical feats by doing an impromptu impersonation of a candle. After he removed a flaming hat from his head, his hair caught fire. Coliseum security was

**Opposite:** "Wild things" Stern and Sam Kinison, live out their long-haired, guitar-slinging, rock and roll fantasy.

# The Former Preacher and the Church Secretary

In the late 1980s, Stern show regulars Jessica Hahn and Sam Kinison became central figures in a riveting psychodramatic radio soap opera. Kinison, a former preacher turned stand-up comic, first came to the public's attention in Rodney Dangerfield's 1985 HBO special. A heavyset man with stringy blond hair, Kinison was known for his outrageous screaming comic tirades. Critics who missed the humor accused Kinison of homophobia, sacrilege, and free-floating hostile insensitivity.

Kinison also became famous for his drug and alcohol exploits. One of Stern's favorite guests, Kinison would often visit the radio show with some chemical or another flowing through his veins. Listeners were thrilled to hear a man on the edge who might do or say anything. Kinison seemed hell-bent on self-destruction.

Jessica Hahn became an instant media sensation for her involvement in a sordid sex scandal with televangelist Jim Bakker. Stern managed to break through the glut of reporters who had descended on Hahn. Representing himself as a concerned party who cared about Hahn's personal welfare, Stern earned her trust and forged a friendship in the middle of the media circus. As manipulative as Stern's maneuver appeared (being in regular contact with a key player at the height of the scandal was a major score), he has since proven himself to be a supportive friend. Hahn returns the favor by participating, often scantily clad in see-through ensembles, at many of Stern's events. Since the scandal, Hahn has undergone extensive plastic surgery and appeared twice in *Playboy*.

Stern's relationships with both these characters had their ups and downs. For a long time Stern and Kinison feuded over a practical joke gone awry. Kinison had promised to reunite Stern with the rock band Bon Jovi, former Stern show regulars who had apparently turned their backs on the disc jockey when they made the big time. The much anticipated on-air reunion never happened and a disappointed Stern became furious with prankster Kinison. Stern and Kinison's on-again, off-again friendship paled in comparison to the Kinison/Hahn love-hate fest.

Following a tabloid-worthy fling, Hahn reported to Stern that a heavily inebriated Kinison had fallen asleep inside her during sexual intercourse. Hahn added the unpleasant detail that a drunk and disoriented Kinison had once defecated on a hotel room carpet. Stern and Hahn recorded a comedy bit spoofing the alleged incident, featuring television's beloved talking horse, Mr. Ed (played by Stern), nodding off while sexually galloping into a passionately accommodating Hahn. Stern then persuaded the two ex-lovers to get together over the telephone on the radio to make up. It turned out to be a battle royal. Kinison's savagely cutting remarks reduced Hahn to tears. Hahn hung up and Stern somehow managed to calm the enraged Kinison. When the air cleared, both men concurred that this was "great radio." It was always great radio with Kinison.

By 1992, Kinison had hit bottom and was beginning to climb out of the well of recklessness and despair. In Alcoholics Anonymous and off drugs, he was making an effort to clean up his act. On April 5, 1992, Kinison married Malika Souri. Tragically, five days later, Kinison was killed in a head-on collision on his way to a sold-out engagement in Laughlin, Nevada. Even in death, Kinison remains a part of Stern's show. On Halloween 1997, the Amazing Kreskin held a seance in the studio and "channeled" the spirit of Kinison through four participants. Kinison (an impersonator, that is) occasionally calls in from hell to report recent arrivals and talk over old times. In 1994, Stern optioned *Brother Sam*, a biography penned by Kinison's brother Bill and Steve Delson, for development into a motion picture. Stern, a friend to the end and beyond, keeps the spirit of Kinison alive.

"*Everybody has different taste and finds different things offensive. That's what the radio dial is for.*"

forced to douse Mazzeo when it appeared as though he was prepared to ignite his entire person. An attempted reconciliation between former lovers Jessica Hahn and comedian Sam Kinison dissolved into a wicked war of words. *Penthouse* Pet Kimberly Taylor, fondling a large cucumber, was unconvincingly hypnotized by Dr. Marshall King to orgasm every time Stern touched his nose. The musical finale of the evening featured Leslie West on lead guitar as Kinison performed "Wild Thing," during which Coliseum security allowed Stern's screaming fans to flood the arena floor and charge the stage. An edited version of *U.S. Open Sores* became Stern's second widely purchased video offering.

Having proven himself a hugely popular entertainer, Stern was only months away from negotiating a television deal. Things were going well—too well. It was the proverbial calm before the storm. In 1992, the FCC, silent for nearly two and a half years, was about to strike again.

## Let's Go to the Tape

The FCC set its sights on Stern and Infinity Broadcasting after receiving complaints from New Jersey listener Anne M. Stommel. Stommel had tuned in to Stern's show in December 1988 and listened in horrific agitation as the upcoming Christmas party was hyped. The Christmas show aired on December 16, 1988, and Stern delivered the wild celebration promised. Among the on-air revelers were lesbians, a gay choir, a hypnotist, strippers, and a unique musical stylist—a man who played the piano with his penis. It was a typically raucous Stern romp. Stommel was not amused and sent transcripts and her homemade tapes of the show to the FCC. Almost a year after the broadcast, Infinity was informed that it was under investigation again.

Infinity and its lawyers vigorously challenged the FCC charges and responded that Stern's show could not be considered "patently offensive" by local or national standards. Infinity maintained that television was packed with talk shows that explored sexuality and bodily functions much more explicitly than Stern ever dared. The response went so far as to cite a study that concluded there were absolutely no unsupervised youngsters listening to Stern. This last claim may have been absurdly impossible to prove, but it was no more ridiculous than that which the FCC considered offensive.

Gary Dell'Abate with cosmetically enhanced teeth and Jessica Hahn.

On December 1, 1990, the FCC, unconvinced by Infinity's defense, imposed a $6,000 fine—$2,000 for each station that aired the Christmas show (in addition to K-Rock and WYSP, Stern was syndicated on WJFK in Washington, D.C., as of October 3, 1988). The FCC charged that the show was "lewd and vulgar," guilty of "dwelling on sexual matters, including sexual intercourse, orgasm, masturbation, lesbianism, homosexuality, breasts, nudity, and male and female genitalia." Karmazin declared that the ruling violated Stern's constitutional right to free speech and vowed to fight the FCC in court if necessary. Years would pass before matters could be resolved between Infinity and the FCC.

Stern was outraged by the double standard whereby "tits and ass" could be discussed seriously on Phil Donahue's television program while the satirist was reprimanded. Stern contended that both he and Donahue explored sexual topics for the same simple reason: ratings. Considering the relative popularity between the two media, it was far more likely that a child would turn on a television before resorting to radio entertainment. Such observations were lost on the FCC. Nonetheless, Stern did manage to extract some gain from the wrongheaded ruling. A double-cassette audiotape, edited from the now infamous Christmas show and titled *Crucified by the FCC*, was direct-marketed to those champions of the First Amendment who had missed out on the fun the first time.

## Saturday Night Vile

Stern's goal to branch out into other media, television in particular, was realized by the summer of 1990. WWOR, based in Secaucus, New Jersey, hired Stern and his crew to put together a weekly show to be aired Saturdays at 11 P.M. Although the production budget was exceedingly meager, as was reflected in the final product, there were distinct advantages to the arrangement. Of primary importance was Stern's complete artistic control. The second significant factor was that WWOR was a superstation (carried on cable systems across the United States)—this was Stern's first real shot at national exposure.

After a test run of four episodes during the summer of 1990, the television incarnation of *The Howard Stern Show* was picked up for national syndication in January 1991. As with radio, on television Stern regularly pushed the limits of what was acceptable. Generally, the hour-long show was edited down from ninety minutes of material presented to WWOR for approval. Stern's cutting-edge television was typical Stern: unbelievable, outrageous, appalling, and undeniably funny.

For a year and a half, Stern reworked many of his radio bits into the visual medium and introduced his viewers to the odd assemblage of personalities intrinsic to his wacky world. Many of the bits were game show spoofs. "Homeless Howiewood Squares" pitted homeless contestants against one another for the grand prize of a shopping cart full of aluminum cans. The secret square offered the promise of a new home: a cardboard refrigerator box. In "Hooker Howiewood Squares," an assortment of genuine prostitutes filled the celebrity squares, and Susan Olsen and Mike Lookinland (better known as television's innocent Cindy and Bobby Brady of *The Brady Bunch*) acted as contestants. Other spoofs included "The Hooker Price Is Right," "The Lesbian Dating Game," and "What's My Secret," wherein panelists Arlene Francis and

Kitty Carlisle Hart (actual game show divas), unable to guess the secret, were shocked to discover that the guest's mystery was lesbianism. They had had no idea what they were in for or even what Stern was all about when they had agreed to do the show, but after the shock, they still managed to maintain their fastidious television guest demeanors, however.

Stern informs the media that he has quit his WWOR Television show to pursue a major motion picture deal.

Notable among the bizarre, surreal, and grotesque novelty acts to appear on the WWOR show were Denise Miller, known as "the Kielbasa Queen" for deep-throating twelve-inch lengths of Polish sausage; Kenneth Keith Kallenbach, whose attempts to blow smoke through his eyes caused him to vomit; Suzanne Muldowney, named "Underdog Lady" for her representation of the named cartoon character; and the vermivorous Vinnie D'Amico, who savored a plate of live worms. Now, that's entertainment!

In the ratings, Stern's television show was a tremendous success—in many markets it easily beat NBC's *Saturday Night Live* from 11:30 P.M. to midnight, the half hour the two shows overlapped. But it was too good to last. Stern was at war with management again and aired his grievances with WWOR on his daily radio show. The insults and hostility Stern directed toward the Secaucus superstation took their toll, and in the summer of 1992 WWOR announced the show's "cancellation." The station indicated that Stern was taken off the air because the production costs exceeded the advertising revenue generated by the show. The bad press threatened Stern's chances for future television gigs. The opinion that Stern lacked the clout to draw advertisers in the minds of television executives could be disastrous. Stern countered the notion and declared that his show was not canceled, but that he was leaving television to pursue adventures on the big screen. Hollywood beckoned.

"The FCC should be more specific of what it is they want us to do."
—Mel Karmazin

**Right:** An animal not found in any zoo, "Stuttering" John Melendez costumed in a monkey suit at an L.A. funeral for rival DJs. **Opposite:** "Stuttering" John Melendez—Stern's stammering verbal terrorist of the rich, famous, and self-important.

# Out-of-Left-Field Reporter

The path from intern on *The Howard Stern Show* to national celebrity interviewer is fraught with rejection, danger, and obstacles—not the least of which is a speech impediment. John Melendez, affectionately known as "Stuttering John," was brought on as an unpaid intern at K-Rock in 1989. Melendez was instantly assigned the unenviable task of asking public figures questions even Stern acknowledges as "degrading, disgusting, and tasteless," presumably because of his spasmodic, repetitive manner of speech. Melendez took to the job like a man possessed, an undeterred investigative journalist who showed no compunction when posing his barrage of embarrassing questions.

Inquiries by the fearless Melendez have included:
• To baseball slugging legend Ted Williams, "Did you ever fart in the catcher's face?"
• To bulimic actress Ally Sheedy, "When was the last time you threw up?"
• To holy man the Dalai Lama, "Do people ever say 'Hello, Dalai'?"
• To celebrity interview queen Barbara Walters, "Do you think other people who talk like Elmer Fudd should pursue a future in journalism?"

During the run of the WWOR television show, Melendez reached the height of his infamy as an out-of-left-field reporter. At the press conference in which Gennifer Flowers was to discuss her alleged twelve-year affair with presidential candidate Bill Clinton, Melendez burst out of the media pack and inquired, "Gennifer, did Governor Clinton use a condom?" and "Will you be sleeping with any other presidential candidates?" Melendez was an overnight sensation, discussed by political pundits and journalists from coast to coast. When the sudden fame appeared to go to Melendez's head, Stern threatened to replace him with an interviewer who suffered from Tourette's syndrome. Fortunately, Melendez prevailed over his afflicted competitor and was rewarded with a salary.

Melendez has suffered for his artlessness, as some angry celebrities have threatened, pushed, shoved, struck, and yelled at the determined inquisitor. Stern admires Melendez's pit bull terrier dedication and has fondly dubbed him "hero of the stupid."

"When I'm on the radio, I can be exactly what I am and say exactly what I feel. I'm role playing in real life. But I can get on the radio and be who I feel I am inside."

# CHAPTER SIX

The King
of All
Media

Stern may not have been a household name by the early 1990s, but his fame was steadily increasing. The public at large was becoming familiar with Stern through television appearances, syndication of his radio show, and the ongoing battle with the FCC. Stern wasted no time promoting his upcoming major motion picture debut. (Stern's only previous foray into the world of cinema was a cameo in

the 1986 low-budget detective spoof *Ryder P.I.* He received a measly $1,000 for his appearance as goofy newscaster Ben Wah.)

On July 27, 1992, *Variety* reported Stern's development deal with New Line and Permut Presentations for an undetermined film project, tentatively titled *Howard Stern: The Movie.* Stern vowed it would be "the most disgusting movie ever made." He and the Hollywood studios had been courting for years, but the ideal project remained elusive. What would be the subject of Stern's movie? During an appearance on *The Tonight Show*, he abruptly answered this question with "Fartman."

Stern originally introduced his alter ego, the fuming caped crusader Fartman, while at DC-101. A defender of democracy who, swift as the broken wind, brought down enemies with his noxious intestinal *arse*nal, Fartman policed the international scene and threatened to *blow away* those

who stood in the way of truth, justice, and the putrid power of his posterior. Fartman was first seen on Stern's WWOR television show paired with Adam West (television's Batman); the "F" emblazoned on his chest appeared at the center of a toilet-seat necklace. Stern's glib remark to Leno was in jest. There were no plans to do a Fartman movie—yet.

Tuning in to *The Tonight Show* that evening was screenwriter Jonathan Lawton, who had penned the highly successful movies *Pretty Woman* and *Under Siege.* Intrigued by Stern's project idea, Lawton contacted New Line and expressed an interest in writing the screenplay. Regarding the odd chain of events, Stern told *Playboy,* "New Line was floored. They didn't want to do *Fartman*—I didn't even want to do *Fartman*—but now there's this guy [Lawton] calling who they would give their left nut to work with."

In September 1992, Fartman descended on the MTV Music Video Awards. The gaseous superhero was lowered to the stage on wires in an outfit designed to expose more buttocks than it concealed. Fartman turned away from his co-presenter, Luke Perry, aimed his backside at the podium, and blasted it away. New Line hoped that Fartman would blow audiences away as well.

By November, Lawton was signed on and *The Adventures of Fartman* was put into development with a projected $8-11 million budget and a May 1993 production start. Lawton told the press, "It has to be as outrageous as Howard is. If we don't offend some people, we won't have done our job." It was a job that went undone, however. Due to disagreements over merchandising, the deal collapsed and the movie went unproduced. In the end, *The Adventures of Fartman* turned out to be what it always was—just a lot of hot air.

## Number One Coast to Coast

Television and movie disappointments aside, Stern was enjoying phenomenal success with his radio show. Stern's renegotiated 1990 contract with Infinity paved the way for his move into the Los Angeles radio market. In July 1991, Infinity agreed to allow Stern's show to broadcast in Los Angeles through a unique arrangement. In an unprecedented business move, Infinity licensed *The Howard Stern Show* to competing station KLSX, owned by Greater Media, Inc.

*(continued on page 92)*

Karmazin acknowledged that everyone benefited financially: "This is a way to expand our revenue without having to buy another radio station." Infinity's move opened the door for licensing in other cities. Additionally, Stern was to be the first local personality in radio history to be simultaneously broadcast in more than one market by stations owned by different companies.

Stern was very eager to go against the City of Angels' reigning morning men, Mark and Brian. Stern told Paul Heine of FMQB, "You've got two morons on the air doing everything that I do. I want a shot a teaching those guys a lesson. And we will teach them a lesson. We will beat them worse than the L.A. police beat Rodney King." The fact that Mark and Brian's popularity had earned them a prime-time television deal with NBC (which was soon dissolved) could only have added fuel to the fire. Stern had his work cut out for him. Mark and Brian at KLOS were number one with a 7.5 rating; KLSX, Stern's Los Angeles outlet, was in twenty-first place with a paltry 1.8 rating.

Luckily, Andy Bloom, the program director who masterminded Stern's import to Philadelphia, had moved on to KLSX. Despite fears that Stern's show was too "East Coast" for laid-back Los Angelenos, Bloom was utterly convinced that Stern would take Los Angeles by storm and climb to the top of the ratings. Bloom told Michael Lev in *The New York Times*, "It's a mismatch. Howard is a comedian of national stature. His competitors are two goofy D.J.'s doing shtick." Ken Barnes, editor of *Radio & Records*, was less optimistic and pondered, "L.A. is the great enigma; it historically has not responded that well to phenomena from other markets, specifically New York." Stern was about to make history.

In October 1992, Stern took over as Los Angeles' number-one morning personality. Funeral rites for Mark and Brian followed quickly. ("First I want to just strip and rape Mark and Brian. I want my two bitches laying there in the cold, naked.") The same month a deal was inked with the E! Network (Entertainment Television) for *The Howard Stern Interview*. The format of the E! show was a half-hour weekly interview in which Stern, without the input of his radio family, grilled his guests about their sex lives, financial situations, and other topics run-of-the-mill interviewers avoided out of deference, respect, and mitigated gall. Stern's third television show, which debuted November 27, 1992, ran for

**Above:** The King of All Media encourages his subjects to express their appreciation during the filming of *Private Parts*.
**Opposite, left:** The Offender and the Pretender: On the television set with rock and roll vocalist and guitar player Chrissie Hynde. **Opposite, right:** Stern's cable television home, E!, which lays claim to being "the only place people can get a complete, inside look at Howard's provocative radio show, six nights a week."

thirty-six episodes before time constraints made the continuation of the L.A.-based *Interview* impossible. Before long, Stern would reappear on E! for his fourth television venture.

Early in 1994, Rick Marin of *Rolling Stone* asked Stern if a taped version of the radio show would work on television. Stern replied, "I don't think that would be the answer. There's a certain intimacy with radio that people like. They like that there's not a camera on them. They tend to admit more and be more open." Toward the end of 1994, Stern had changed his tune. (A reported $33,000 per episode may have been a compelling factor.) E! worked out a multicamera (seven studio cameras and a handheld Hi 8 camera for guest response upon entering and leaving the studio) arrangement whereby virtually everything that goes on during the radio broadcast is captured on tape. The hours of daily footage are edited into "suitable for television" half-hour segments, which premiere weeknights at 11 P.M. Stern conceded, "After the first couple of days we forgot the cameras were there."

Evidently Stern's guests are not intimidated by the presence of cameras, as the facile interviewer has no difficulty eliciting unexpected confessions and surprising revelations. Stern's show receives the highest ratings of any show on E! Stern claims to never watch his show on the one-hundred-inch television in the basement retreat of his Long Island home. The reason? "My local cable system doesn't carry E!"

"The success of Howard Stern is a reflection of the public's unhealthy fascination with sex, violence, and disrespect."

—A. Larry Ross, president of a Christian public relations firm

## His Kind of Town Chicago Ain't

Now that Stern ruled both coasts, it was time to hit the nation's third-largest radio market: Chicago. The lucrative licensing of Stern's show had worked out quite nicely for Infinity and a deal was cut with Evergreen Media Corp., owner of Chicago's WLUP AM/FM, "the Loop." Vice president and general manager of WLUP Lawrence J. Wert first contacted Buchwald with a confidential overnight dispatch and preliminary offer on January 15, 1992. Wert assured Buchwald that Stern was WLUP's "number one choice" for the morning slot and that the station was anxious get him on the air before the spring ratings book. Wert confided that he was intent on avoiding a "bidding war" (other Chicago stations had expressed an interest in Stern). Negotiations dragged on until Buchwald was satisfied with the terms of the agreement.

A well-compensated Stern hit the Chicago airwaves on October 15, 1992. Soon thereafter, Stern's eager suitors prematurely lost their ardor for the keenly courted morning man. The honeymoon ended on August 30, 1993—less than a year into the relationship. The actual reasoning behind WLUP's termination of the contract was never satisfactorily explained to Stern, Buchwald, or Infinity. The excuse that potential FCC violations made Evergreen uneasy seemed highly unlikely. Evergreen's declaration—"This is not the type of programming which we can or will purchase, nor is it what was contemplated by the express terms of our agreement"—appeared to be a patent falsehood considering their initial correspondence with Buchwald: "We are familiar with Howard's program." Most probably, Evergreen was "familiar" with Stern's high ratings and consequent revenue boosting power. Stern's failure to prove himself in the ratings (ten months was hardly a fair gauge of his potential appeal) was certainly a contributing factor in Wert's decision.

Stern filed a lawsuit against WLUP for breach of contract and proceeded to attack his former Chicago employers on the air. Stern had good reason to believe that a WLUP-orchestrated campaign to poison his name not only injured him in Chicago but was damaging him in other radio markets. He maintained that deals fell through in both Miami and Phoenix as a result of his Chicago cancellation. On top of it all, Stern was bad-mouthed by WLUP's on-air

personalities as a "failure" and another Chicago disc jockey, Mancow Muller, had sent Stern a package containing excrement. Stern directed his venom at Wert: "I wish AIDS on you, and I wish AIDS on your family." Stern sued Evergreen for millions of dollars in damages (Stern calculated his financial loss to be a minimum of $3.1 million), but the greatest injury was to his pride and reputation.

Stern returned to the Chicago airwaves in 1995. WKCG picked up Stern's show only to drop it within six months. Infinity-owned WJJD moved in quickly and added Stern to their programming lineup. At last Stern was able to go head-to-head with all of the Chicago personalities who had mocked him in his absence. Muller deservedly received the brunt of Stern's savagery and was eventually chased out of the Chicago radio market.

**Right:** At a press conference, Stern stuns the literary world and announces his book deal with Simon & Schuster.

**Opposite:** At a book signing Stern momentarily puts down the pen to hold up a copy of *Private Parts*. In some instances it was calculated that Stern produced nearly 900 signatures an hour!

## Man of (More than Four) Letters

Stern had accumulated a great deal of material to discuss on his daily radio show: mounting FCC fines for "indecency"; promotion of his latest video, *Butt Bongo Fiesta*; and the birth of his third daughter, Ashley Jade, on January 24, 1993. Stern's fans savored every detail of his personal and professional life as Stern turned the prosaic into a daily comedic rant and rave. And he was about to give them more—a book.

Stern's literary venture, urged by Buchwald, was designed to erase the residual negative impressions that had followed the collapse of the Fartman project. Buchwald remarked, "There was a perception that he had taken a hit, that Howard had somehow failed at the movies. So we thought of the book as something that would both produce income and suggest to people that Howard had economic clout." That same month, Buchwald put a deal together with Simon & Schuster. Larry "Ratso" Sloman would help Stern find his "voice" on paper, and Judith Regan would be the editor. Stern dedicated himself to producing a manuscript and completed the freewheeling, anecdotal autobiography, *Private Parts* (Stern's proposed titles rejected by Simon & Schuster included *Howard Stern's Penis*, *Mein Kampf*, and *I, Moron*), in time for publication in the fall. The so-called intelligentsia and literary elite doubted Stern's fans could read, much less be counted on to pay $23 for a tome by their hero, the blue-tongued devil. They were in for a surprise.

Within hours of going on sale on October 7, *Private Parts* had sold out. A remarkable 225,000 copies were instantly snatched up, and within two weeks, *Private Parts* was in its eighth printing with more than a million copies in print (based on a the standard 15 percent royalty rate, Stern was expected to clear approximately $3.5 million).

Stern rocketed to the top of the best-seller lists. (Some squeamish retailers refused to carry the book, going so far as to deny its number one position by altering *The New York Times* best-seller list.) The controversy surrounding the publication and distribution of *Private Parts* was easily overshadowed by record-breaking sales. At book signings across the nation, thousands of Stern's fans lined the streets in hopes of obtaining an autographed copy of the fastest-selling book in Simon & Schuster's history.

During the opening production number of *The Miss Howard Stern New Year's Eve Pageant*, the King ascends to the stage on a porcelain throne.

Stern was given his due as an undeniable literary giant. The self-proclaimed King of All Media ruled the realm of the printed word.

Suddenly, radio's bad boy, now a massively successful, critically acclaimed author, was the darling of the mainstream media. He was not about to rest on his laurels. Aspirations for future television and/or movie ventures prompted Stern to further prove his "commercial viability." Stern's next move was a pay-per-view extravaganza, *The Miss Howard Stern New Year's Eve Pageant*. Stern sought to capitalize on the purchasing power of his growing base of fans. Historically, pay-per-view entertainment events fared poorly, but Stern's two-hour year-end salute to the sophomoric, salacious, and silly was another story.

# Adventures in the Third Dementia

Stern had good reason to suspect that *The Miss Howard Stern New Year's Eve Pageant*, priced at $39.95, would be a huge success. By the end of 1993, the stock of Stern's *Butt Bongo Fiesta* was sold out—260,000 units were purchased for $39.45 each.

For fans of Stern's canceled WWOR television show, *Butt Bongo Fiesta* filled a void. The videotape offered the sort of material definitely not suitable for broadcast television. In a 3-D segment (two pairs of 3-D glasses were provided with the videocassette), Stern as "Jungleman" conquers the "big, sloppy, naked titty women" and rescues damsel in distress Jessica Hahn. Stern's Jungleman character evidently suffered the same irritable bowel syndrome as Fartman, for upon freeing the bound Hahn, an engulfing "three-dimensional" cloud of green gas escaped from beneath the jungle hero's loincloth.

Other segments included "Guess Who's the Jew" with Daniel Carver, "the KKK Guy," as a panelist (Stern often plays Carver's hideously racist recorded hotline messages on the radio show); "Lesbian Love Connection"; the notorious Captain Janks/Annette DeBella date; and winners of the "Gross Video Contest." For those who enjoyed the WWOR "Tribute to Breasts" episode, there was "Tribute to the Vagina." The actual "Butt Bongo" was fittingly saved for the tail end of the presentation.

*Butt Bongo Fiesta* was vintage Stern—an oddly amusing journey into the realm of bad taste, taboos, and juvenilia. Stern would outdo himself with the New Year's Eve "pageant," thought by critics to be the most disgusting, outrageous television "entertainment" ever.

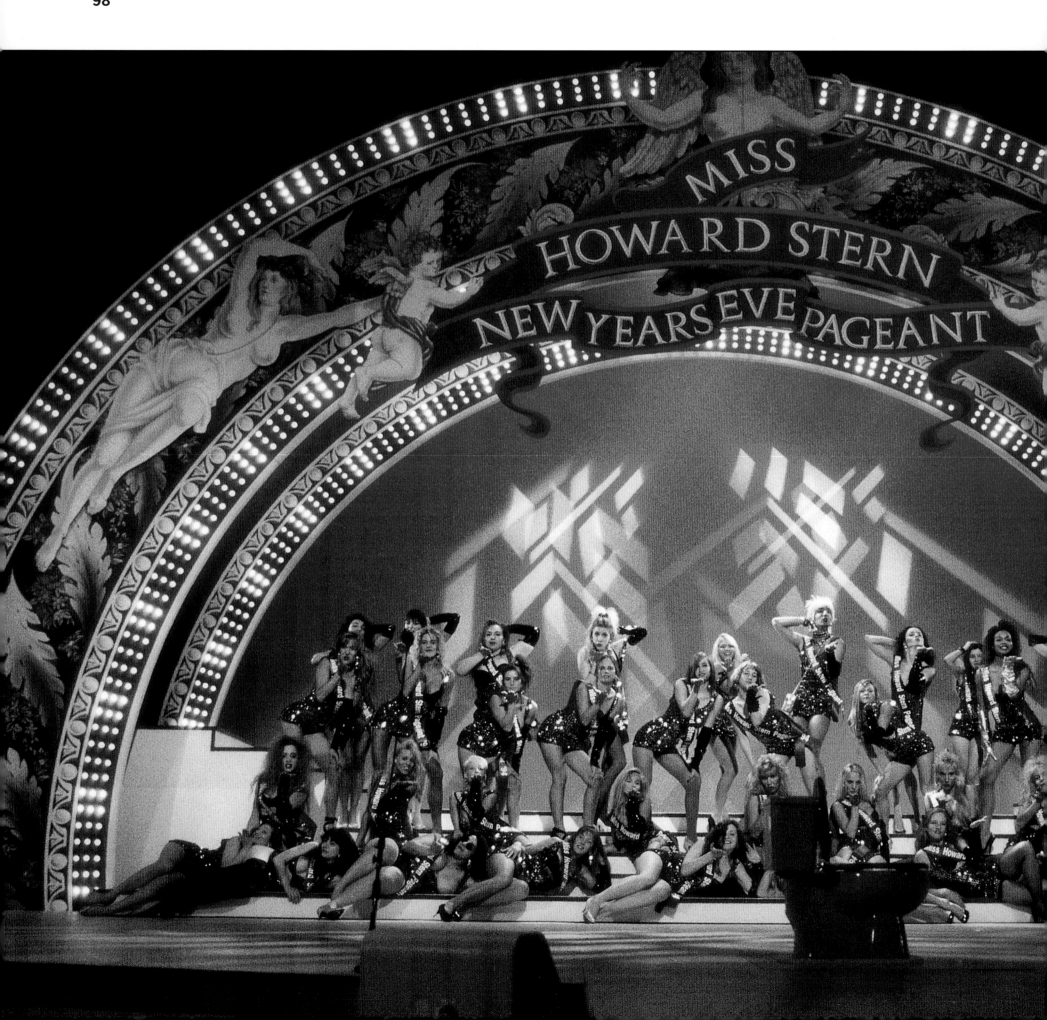

Stern's end-of-year bash, held at Newark, New Jersey's Symphony Hall, pulled out all the stops. Although preparations for the "pageant" had been under way since early November, the show at times approached the excitement of something madly improvised. The event's musical director, Bob Stein, confided the reason for this: Stern preferred to keep rehearsal to a minimum, thus maintaining a professional but spontaneous vitality. The show included appearances by real artists such as singer Janis Ian, tabloid media star John Wayne Bobbitt, and pageant contestants included a topless, maggot-eating lass (Ian assured those disgusted by the display that the competing omnivore ate more in rehearsal) and an opera singer who lost consciousness during an airless aria performed with a plastic bag over her head. Purchased by at least 348,000 cable subscribers, Stern's "pageant" became the highest-grossing pay-per-view entertainment event in history. For some it was an evening to remember; for others it was an evening they could not forget.

## Backlash and Forward

Prior to New Year's Eve, Stern assured the media he was unconcerned that fallout from the pay-per-view special "that might be perceived as blue or raunchy" would jeopardize his newfound mass-market legitimacy. Bill Carter of *The New York Times* reported Stern's reaction to projections of potential backlash: "I have never gotten anywhere worrying about the powerful elite who run the media, the people who might be looking at me for late-night television or movies or things like that. I go by what I think is funny. When it comes to pay-per-view I know who I have to satisfy."

Stern may not have worried about the powerful elite, but they were clearly worried about him. By the end of January 1994, Judy Brennan of *The Los Angeles Times* reported that the special "went too far for Twentieth Century-Fox mogul Rupert Murdoch, whose TV group was seriously considering Stern to replace the short-lived late-night Chevy Chase show." Stern's opportunity to break into the late-night arena vanished. (It is doubtful that a late-night show would have panned out for Stern. The workload that was required to record a television show in the evening after his morning radio show was prohibitive, if not impossible.) Paramount Pictures also jumped off the careening Stern bandwagon—

In more ways than one, *The Miss Howard Stern New Year's Eve Pageant* was the highest *grossing*, nonsports pay-per-view event in history.

plans to produce a low-budget adaptation of *Private Parts* were dropped.

It was widely believed that Stern was persona non grata in Hollywood circles, but on May 23, 1994, the film industry trade publications reported that Rysher Entertainment and Stern had agreed to bring *Private Parts* to the big screen with a projected $15 million budget. Part of Stern's agreement with Rysher gave him script approval or, more to the point, script disapproval. For almost two years Stern repeatedly rejected script after script—none of which accurately captured the spirit of Stern or his autobiographical opus. Rysher suspected that the radio star had cold feet and suggested that actor Jeff Goldblum portray Stern. Stern would not let that happen—Stern's fans wanted to see Stern onscreen, not some actor. Originally scheduled for a summer 1995 release, *Private Parts* looked like it might go the way of *The Adventures of Fartman*. In the meantime, Stern had set his sights on other arenas.

**Opposite, far left:** The poster for the critically acclaimed, commercially successful film version of Stern's autobiography, *Private Parts*. **Opposite, center:** On the set of *Private Parts*, Stern gives the crew a glimpse of his unusual undergarment—a strapless bra! **Left:** Stern with Angus Young, a member of the band AC/DC, during the shooting of *Private Parts*. **Below:** Fear and loathing on the campaign trail 1994: Libertarian candidate Stern addresses the press.

## The Political Animal

In addition to advertisers, radio station owners, and media analysts, Stern's phenomenal popularity has been a source of great interest to another special self-interest group—politicians. Stern had a long-standing policy regarding political endorsement; whichever candidate called in first won the widely heard morning man's support. In 1993, New Jersey Republican gubernatorial candidate Christine Todd Whitman beat the competition to the phone. Stern's support of Whitman's candidacy is believed to have been instrumental in her narrow defeat of incumbent governor Jim Florio. (Whitman showed her appreciation by fulfilling her promise to name a New Jersey rest stop after Stern. Located on I-295 in Burlington County, an eight-and-a-half-by eleven-inch aluminum plaque, produced at a cost of $1,000 in private funds, marked the spot's January 1995 dedication. The plaque was subsequently stolen and mailed to Stern.)

Libertarian Party member Robert Goodman from the Bronx had been sending Stern information on his political party from 1985. Familiar with Stern's "first call first served" policy, Goodman encouraged his friend, Libertarian candidate for New York governor Gary Johnson, to call Stern during his 1990 campaign. Johnson won Stern's endorsement and received 24,611 votes.

Four years later, Stern heard from the Libertarians again for support of a different variety. Stern had been railing against Governor Mario Cuomo on-air for months and threatened to run against Cuomo in the upcoming election. Goodman was in touch again, encouraging Stern to run as the Libertarian candidate. After a brief courtship, Stern agreed to throw his hat in the ring. On March 22, 1994, Stern announced his intention to run against Cuomo. New Yorkers were in for an interesting race.

The first order of business was for Stern to win the party nomination at their convention in Albany, on April 23 and 24. The Libertarian's state party chairman, Ludwig Vogel, was delighted and instructed Stern that if he could fill the convention with supporters he would be a shoe-in to garner a two-thirds majority vote. Stern mobilized his fans to become registered Libertarians by April 8 and pack the convention. Stern's run for governor offered distinct advantages to the Libertarians: the party's coffers would

"I'm sure I'm filled with inconsistencies, but fuck that, I'm not president of the United States."

More caper than Capra: "Mr. Stern Goes to Albany," was a wonderfully amusing exercise in crossing politics with performance art.

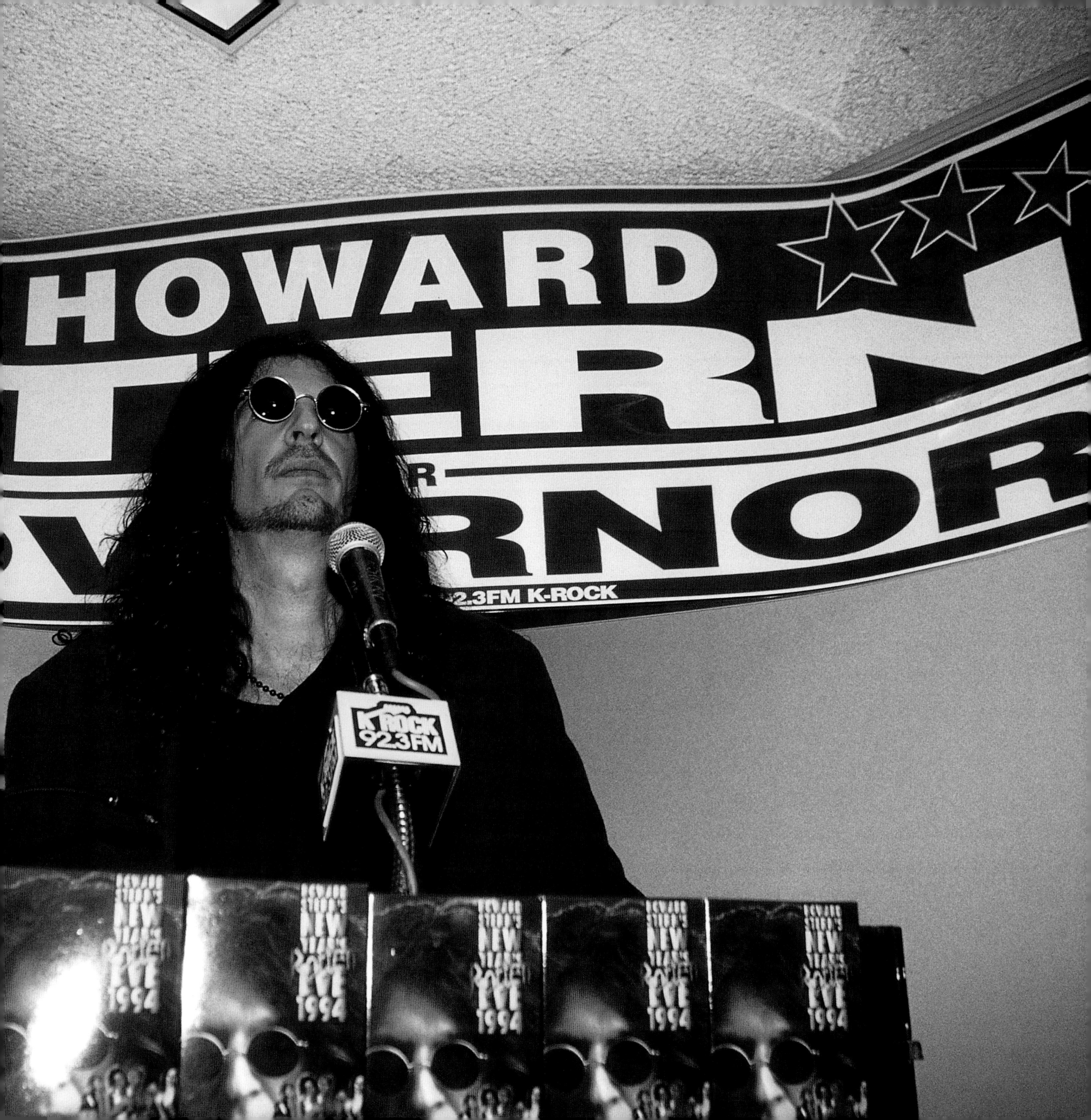
HOWARD
K ROCK
92.3FM

be enriched (new members were required to pay a $15 fee), and if Stern won fifty thousand votes, the Libertarians would be granted permanent ballot status. Vogel enthused, "I think this could become a win-win situation for us." Unconvinced and more than a little peeved was the party's would-be candidate, James Ostrowski, who bitterly remarked, "It's making the party look like a joke." Ostrowski refused to accept Stern's "groupies" as true Libertarians and threatened to challenge their right to vote. Don Buchwald remained the supportive "super-agent" and averred, "The man says he's going to be governor, then he's going to be governor." All Stern had to do was overcome the obstacles blocking the path to the governor's mansion.

Talk swiftly and carry a big shtick—
Candidate Stern is "Incorrectly Political."

Stern easily overcame the first hurdle and won the party's nomination, with 287 of the 381 votes cast. In typical Stern fashion, the entire journey to Albany, along with whistle stops at a strip club, was recorded for broadcast. Stern's hand-picked running mate for lieutenant governor was Stan Dworkin, a Rockland County leather goods manufacturer. Stern had a ticket and a forceful three-point platform: road repair would occur at night, the death penalty would be reinstated (proclaimed by the catchy slogan "A Volt for Every Vote!"), and Stern would resign after accomplishing points one and two, at which point Dworkin would take over as Governor.

Stern seemed to have no difficulties with the political and legal impediments that stood before him. And he was

able to get around the FCC's equal-time requirements, which could have forced Stern's show off the air during the gubernatorial race. However, Stern had not foreseen certain obligatory disclosures required of all candidates for governor. The two sticking points were a declaration of residence and a financial statement, which would become a matter of public record. Stern avoided revealing his actual home address by reporting an alternate residence as his permanent domicile. He had no desire to divulge his income.

Stern's request that the state supreme court issue an injunction against the financial disclosure requirement was denied on August 3. Two days later Stern dropped out of the race. (A glib Stern assured those who still might want throw some support his way, "I am resigning from the campaign. I am stepping aside, but I will run for Pope.") Stern contended that the policy was "especially invasive to someone like me who lives a highly visible life." When pressed for his reasons, the frustrated politico retorted, "I spend twenty-five hours a week telling you all the most intimate details of my life. One fact I've never revealed is how much money I have.... It's none of your business."

In an interview with *New York Magazine*'s Maer Roshan, Stern clarified that his reluctance to reveal his income had to do with what he perceived as society's prevalent "class hatred." Stern summed up the problem: "Money is the great divide in our country. I realize it makes people uptight, so I just avoid it."

In the same interview, Stern commented that "what was so great about running for governor was that everything that politicians do behind your back I did in front of you....When I had to have backroom dealings, I had it in front of the audience....I basically told people whatever it is they wanted to hear....It was outrageous." Stern agreed that his campaign was a form of "performance art." Those idealists stunned by Stern's admission that his campaign was more shtick than serious could have spared themselves disillusionment had they read Stern's *Playboy* interview, published shortly after he announced his candidacy, in which he declared: "It's hard to take my politics seriously when I say I'll endorse the first gubernatorial candidate who calls in to the show.... It's all sort of frivolous and fun. Anybody who would be influenced by my goofiness has a mental problem."

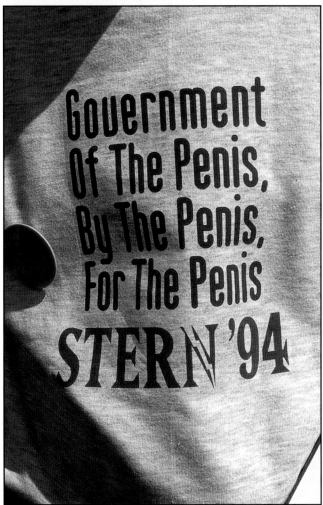

**Top:** A Howard Stern fan stands beside his promotional trailer.
**Left:** A Stern fan's shirt declares a desire for mid-level *organization* of government.

In the last days of September, Stern threw his support to the republican candidate for governor, George Pataki, who like citizen Stern endorsed the reinstatement of the death penalty and nighttime roadwork. When he won the election, Pataki profusely thanked Stern on-air for his support. As a further indication of his appreciation, Pataki provided Stern and his wife with two of the best seats at the governor-elect's swearing-in ceremony on January 1, 1995. Stern had made it to the governor's mansion after all.

## A Fine Contribution

In November 1992, Stern and Infinity were smacked with massive fines by the one-man anti-Stern campaign of the FCC Las Vegas resident, Al Westcott, which resulted in an unprecedented $105,000 fine. The most publicized of the thirty-nine remarks Westcott cited as offensive was Stern's admission that "the closest I came to making love to a black woman was masturbating to a picture of Aunt Jemima on a pancake box." (Fortunately, the Trademark and Patent Office did not charge Stern with "trademark violation.")

In December, Infinity was hit with another $600,000 fine (the FCC backed down from barring Infinity's $100 million purchase of three radio stations). Free speech advocates cried that the FCC's intimidation was too much; groups like Morality in Media insisted it was not enough. A year later, the fines had risen to $1.2 million and the commission took a stronger position by delaying Infinity's $170 million purchase of three more radio stations.

By 1995, the FCC's fines had mounted to $1.7 million. Stern's friends in high places could do nothing to get the commission off his back. Former New York City mayor Edward I. Koch commented: "I think that the FCC was very unfair to Howard Stern. When you see what takes place on television in terms of violence and sex, and then compare that with the occasional scatological, clever comment by Howard Stern you say, 'Why would they try to drive him off the air?'"

The dispute was settled in September 1995. Infinity did not admit to any wrongdoing but made a "voluntary contribution to the U.S. Treasury" of $1,715,000. Infinity declared that the settlement "normalized" their relationship with the FCC. Presumably the commission would stop its efforts to delay approval of Infinity's expansion plans. Infinity's lawyer, Steven Lerman, declared, "The settlement removes a cloud over the company when it comes to our dealings with the agency." But the clouds would return, and the FCC continues to practice its government-sanctioned extortion against Stern and his employers to this day.

"If I ever worried about my image, I'd be in big trouble, because everything I say is wrong. So I find the phoniness in show business pathetic."

Stern sees one of the major campaign promises of his aborted run for governor come to pass. New York Governor George Pataki signs an overnight highway construction bill into law as Stern looks on.

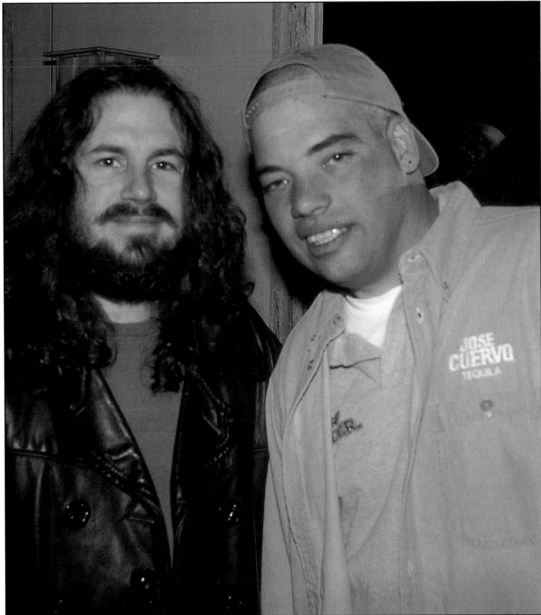

## Fan is Short for Fanatic

No matter how much Stern manipulates and tweaks the media, he occasionally finds himself part of a story he has not devised. Stern has become so widely known that his influence is often unpredictable but almost always fascinating. Herewith is a small sample of news stories involving Stern, his fans, and his enemies:

•In November 1994, Weslaco, Texas, librarian Pam Antonelli lost her job for ordering *Private Parts* for the local library. Stern supported Antonelli by joining her on *Donahue*.

•On December 8, 1994, around 8:10 A.M., Emilio Bonilla, a suicidal twenty-nine-year-old Bronx man, called Stern from his cellular phone as he prepared to jump from the George Washington Bridge. Commuters on the bridge, tuned in to Stern's show, pulled over to borrow Bonilla's phone so that they could chat with Stern. Stern kept Bonilla on the phone until Port Authority police arrived.

•On March 16, 1995, the promotions director for a Cleveland radio station and her boyfriend were charged with disrupting a public service when they pulled the plug on the local competition, which carried Stern's show.

**Opposite:** A book signing for *Private Parts* packed the streets of New York City with thousands of Stern fans. For hours, miserable Manhattan traffic was even worse.
**Above, left:** A Stern fan shows part of her unique autograph collection.
**Above, right:** "Stuttering" John Melendez and "Crackhead" Bob.

•On April 3, 1995, Stern enraged the National Hispanic Media Coalition and fans of murdered Tejano singing sensation Selena by adding gunshot sound effects to recordings of her music on the day of her burial. A warrant for Stern's arrest for disorderly conduct stands in Harlingen, Texas. Stern refused to apologize for his perceived insensitivity but did offer a prepared statement (translated into Spanish) in which he declared that his remarks were meant as satire.

•On April 18, 1996, thirty-two-year-old, Buffalo, New York, resident Samuel L. Callea was charged with third-degree burglary and weapons possession. Disappointed that Stern went off the air in Buffalo, Callea felt "let down in some way." Callea made death threats and followed Stern into the 58th Street garage at 5:30 A.M. as Stern was on his way to work. Callea was harboring a stolen shotgun in the trunk of his car.

"Anybody who sponsors his program should be tarred and feathered."

—Robert Peters, president of Morality in Media

## The King Ascends to the Throne

On November 7, 1995, Stern offered the public another magnum opus. Titled *Miss America* (representatives of the Miss America beauty pageant protested Stern's use of the title), Stern appeared in drag as a thoroughly trashed beauty queen on the book's cover. The rapid sales of Stern's second book proved that the huge success of *Private Parts* was no fluke. By the end of the first week, *Miss America* had sold more copies than Colin Powell's and O.J. Simpson's eagerly awaited literary offerings combined. Book signings attended by swarms of thousands of Stern fans followed.

Similar in tone and content to his first book, *Miss America* revealed an unseen facet of Stern's personality. Stern detailed how he overcame a crippling twenty-year obsessive-compulsive disorder. Stern had touched on the problem in chapter one of *Private Parts* in which he states, quite (continued on page 114)

**Left:** Stern in drag towers above the other girls in a promotion for his second book, *Miss America.*

**Following pages:** From buff to Buffy—the Howard Stern *Miss America* promotional juggernaut plows forward.

"*I think the advertisers are buying a known quantity. When they buy Howard Stern, they know what they are buying, and if an advertiser is comfortable with being involved with a racist, a misogynist and anti-Semite, then Ok.*"

—Terry Rakolta, leader of Americans for Responsible Television

directly, "I confess. I'm an obsessive-compulsive, anal-retentive, miserable neurotic." Following the publication of *Miss America*, Stern told Maer Roshan, "I was going to write about it in my first book. But I think that for the first time in my life, I was embarrassed." Once again, Stern had proven his financial viability. Stern's fans represented a much wider demographic than suspected, with deeper pockets than imagined. Surely they would pay to see Stern in a major motion picture.

On February 14, 1996, the trades reported that Rysher had lost the rights to *Private Parts*. Ivan Reitman (*Ghostbusters, Kindergarten Cop*) stepped in as producer and Stern was back in business with Paramount, in conjunction with Northern Lights. (Curiously, Rysher remained attached to the project as financier.) A screen adaptation of the book *Private Parts* had been penned by Len Blum, who had worked with Reitman on *Meatballs* and *Beethoven's 2nd*. Betty Thomas (*The Brady Bunch Movie*) was signed on as director, and principal photography commenced in May in New York City. Stern was finally going to make his big-screen debut. But was the world ready for Howard Stern, movie star?

The answer to the question was an unqualified YES! No doubt Stern's endless hyping of his movie helped pack the theaters for the March 7, 1997, opening, but *Private Parts'* initial weekend take of $15.1 million proved that Stern represented a major box-office draw. Audiences responded positively to the film (test audiences scored *Private Parts* higher than *Forrest Gump* and *Raiders of the Lost Ark*), which was hailed favorably by film critics as well. The film's soundtrack debuted at number one, and when released on video, *Private Parts* debuted in the top-ten video rentals nationwide.

As for the title "King of All Media," Stern told *TV Guide*, "I never believed it. I was goofing on Michael Jackson calling himself King of Pop." Stern had a number one comedy film, a top-rated radio show (so free of restraints that his contract allows him to run overtime and sign off at his discretion), a popular television show, and two of the fastest-selling books in the history of the written word—if Stern didn't believe in his title, his loyal subjects did. Their slavish devotion to the ubiquitous Stern seems to cry, "Long live the King of All Media."

**Opposite, left:** Howard Stern promotes his latest literary feat with a few scantily clad fans. **Opposite, right:** At a book signing in Los Angeles, Stern takes a break to hold up a copy of his second bestseller, *Miss America*.

Howard holds his Blockbuster
Entertainment Award for Best
Newcomer...backwards.

# A Final Word

As of early 1998, Stern's reign as King of All Media shows no sign of ending anytime soon. Stern's radio show is currently heard in nearly fifty markets, with new stations being added regularly. A promised Howard Stern Radio Network may be in the not-too-distant future. Stern, in association with the CBS Television Stations Group, has announced plans to challenge NBC's long-running *Saturday Night Live* with a show of his own. *The Howard Stern Show*, scheduled to hit the airwaves by the Summer of 1998, promises to draw from the best of the *Howard Stern Radio Show* while developing original content for the Saturday night television comedy contender. In his characteristic mix of candor and irony, splitting the difference between self-promotion and self-deprecation, Stern assured the press, "Late night television is ready for someone like me. The fact of the matter is that standards have gone to an all-time low and I'm here to represent it." Media watchers anticipate the debut of Stern's show will make ratings history. Stern is a fixture in the multimedia landscape with radio, television, and movie deals lined up far into the millennium. Stern's popularity proceeds unabated as the onetime misfit kid from Long Island continues to earn millions of dollars and fans.

Curiosity as to whom Stern really is, the raunchy radio personality or the devoted family man, persists. The electronic media allow for peculiar, usually erroneous assumptions. Stern's fans and enemies presume to "know" Stern and proceed to dissect and psychoanalyze a man with whom they imagine a false, or at best selective, familiarity. A cruise down the information superhighway provides endless information and updates on Stern the man, the myth,

"*I couldn't give a shit about what the audience's reaction is going to be. I just hope they keep tuning in.*"

the media phenomenon. It is only fair to allow Stern the last word on the matter: "People say, 'Well, who's the real guy then?' And I think that the real guy is, you know we all have different facets of our personalities. What you hear on the radio is really me. It's all my beliefs, it's all the things I feel, it's what I think is fun."

Millions of Stern fans agree it's just fun. For those who are not laughing, Stern has this to say: "There are people out there who take life way too seriously because they are too dumb to get the joke."

Perhaps Stern's underlying message can be found in the quotation "Life's a joke—so you may as well laugh."

Additionally, Stern was honored with a Blockbuster Entertainment Award (billed as the "largest publically voted awards show") as Best Male Newcomer in motion pictures for his work in "Private Parts." Stern made the awards ceremony (broadcast on March 10, 1998) uniquely his own by leaping upon the award's presenter, Heather Locklear, and sending her tumbling to the floor locked in his ardent embrace. Stern's acceptance speech also departed from the norm of backslapping ingratiation common to Hollywood award's shows and tended toward face-slapping ingratitude—he thanked no one. However, following the ceremony he did acknowledge and thank the movie's production team.

The King of All Media and his Queen at the Trump/Maples wedding at The Plaza Hotel in New York City.

## BiBLiOGRaPHY

### BOOKS

Cegielski, Jim. *The Howard Stern Book: An Unauthorized, Unabashed, Uncensored Fan's Guide*. New York: Carol Publishing Group, 1994.

Colford, Paul D. *Howard Stern: King of All Media*. New York: St. Martin's Press, 1996, 1997.

Lucaire, Luigi. *Howard Stern A to Z*. New York: St. Martin's Press, 1997.

Quivers, Robin. *Quivers*. New York: HarperCollins Publishers, Inc., 1995.

Stern, Howard. *Private Parts*. New York: Simon & Schuster, Inc., 1993, 1994.

——. *Miss America*. New York: HarperCollins Publishers, Inc., 1995.

Tinker, Grant & Rukeyser, M.S.. *Tinker in Television: From General Sarnoff to General Electric*. New York: Simon & Schuster, Inc., 1994.

### NEWSPAPERS, MAGAZINES, PERIODICALS

"The Aftermath Of Indecency Ruling." *Broadcasting*, April 27, 1987.

Alexander, Max. *Variety*, December 27, 1993.

Anderson, Susan Heller. "Radio Show Cancelled." *The New York Times*, November 20, 1986.

——. "Stern's Station Rebuts F.C.C. Charges." *The New York Times*, December 22, 1986.

Andrews, Edmund L. "Howard Stern Is The Object Of F.C.C. Fine." *The New York Times*, October 28, 1992.

——. "F.C.C. Torn Over Howard Stern Case." *The New York Times*, November 27, 1992.

——. "Howard Stern Employer Faces $600,000 Fine." *The New York Times*, December 18, 1992.

——. "2 Views Of Decency." *The New York Times*, December 28, 1992.

——. "F.C.C. Delays Radio Deals By Howard Stern's Employer." *The New York Times*, December 31, 1993.

Barron, James. "Stores Shy Away From Book Written By Radio Personality." *The New York Times*, November 12, 1993.

Bauder, David. "Howard Stern To Take On 'SNL.'" *The Associated Press*, April 1, 1998.

Beck, Marilyn. *Long Beach Press-Telegram*, January 6, 1993.

Belkin, Lisa. "Some Radio Hosts Flout F.C.C. Obscenity Ruling." *The New York Times*, April 22, 1987.

Bland, Elizabeth L. & Smilgis, Martha. "Shock Jock." *Time*, November 30, 1992.

Boliek, Brooks. "Radio Free America?" *The Hollywood Reporter*, November 22, 1993.

Brennan, Judy. "Stern's New Year's Party Fallout." *The Los Angeles Times*, January 30, 1994.

Bryant, Adam. "Radio Boss Is Undaunted By Big Fine." *The New York Times*, December 21, 1992.

Carter, Bill. "Television." *The New York Times*, December 13, 1993.

Castro, Peter. "A Stern Upbringing." *People Weekly*, November 1, 1993.

Cohen, Rich. "Howard Does Hollywood." *Rolling Stone*. March 20, 1997.

Colford, Paul D. "Now Stern's The King Of All Internet Sites." *The Los Angeles Times*, March 10, 1997.

Cox, Meg. "Howard Stern's Autobiography Is Instant Bestseller." *The Wall Street Journal*, October 15, 1993.

Davis, Bob. "FCC, In Surprise Move, Says It Will Fine Broadcasters For Indecent Programming." *The Wall Street Journal*, April 17, 1987.

Errico, Marcus. "Julia And Will Clean Up At Blockbuster Awards." *E! Online*, March 11, 1998.

Fine, Marshall. "Playboy Interview: Howard Stern." *Playboy*, April 1994.

Fleming, Michael. "Stern's Star Turn." *Variety*, March 3, 1997.

Flood, Alexandra. "Magna Cum Mensch." *The Improper Bostonian*, March 12-25, 1997.

"Going Out Guide." *The New York Times*, October 1, 1985.

Goldberg, Harold. "Putting The E! In Stern." *The Hollywood Reporter*, May 5, 1995.

Goldman, Kevin. "Stern's Sponsors Don't Touch That Dial." *The Wall Street Journal*, December 21, 1992.

Goodman, Walter. "Stern's Complaint." *The New York Times Book Review*, November 14, 1993.

Gross, Jane. "For 'Radio's Bad Boy,' This Isn't Prime Time." *The New York Times*, October 5, 1985.

Handelman, Daniel. "Howard Stern In Private." *TV Guide*, March 8-14, 1997

Heine, Paul. "Up Close! Howard!" *FMQB*, July 12, 1991.

Hoffman, Jan. "Howard Stern Just Won't Shut Up." *New York*, November 18, 1985.

"Howard Stern To Join Radio Station WXRK." *The New York Times*, November 8, 1985.

Kendall, Hamilton & Fleming, Charles. "Ring Out The Old, Gross Out The New." *Newsweek*, January 17, 1994.

Kunen, James S. "Howard Stern: New York's mad-dog deejay may be the mouth of the '80s; he's leader of the pack that's made radio raunchy." *People Weekly*, October 22, 1984.

Lev, Michael. "Big Radio Gamble in the West: Howard Stern." *The New York Times*, August 19, 1991.

Lipton, Michael & Dodd, Johnny. "Stern Rebuke." *People Weekly*, November 16, 1992.

Malanowski, Jamie. "Brace Yourself For Howiewood." *Playboy*, April 1997.

Marin, Rick. "Man or Mouth?" *Rolling Stone*, February 10, 1994.

Marx, Andy. *Variety*, November 25, 1992.

Maryles, Daisy. "Crown Him King." *Publishers Weekly*, November 20, 1995.

McNichol, Tom. "Why Rude and Crude Still Sells." *The Outlook*, March 7-9, 1997.

McShane, Larry. "A Stern Look." *The Daily Breeze*, October 31, 1993.

Mills, Joshua. "He Keeps Giving New Meaning To Gross Revenue." *The New York Times*, October 24, 1993.

Mirabella, Alan. "Good Morning Dog Breath." *New York Daily News*, June 8, 1986.

"Morning Report." *The Los Angeles Times*, August 4, 1994.

Mundaca, Marie. "Kurt Jr. Rubs Salt Into U.S. Open Sores." *Earthdog News*, November 1989.

Pareles, Jon. "Shock Jocks Shake Up Uncle Sam." *The New York Times*, November 15, 1992.

Peterson, Iver. "Shock Jock Is Rewarded For His Political Support." *The New York Times*, January 27, 1995.

"Proust Questionnaire." *Vanity Fair*, March 1997.

Purdum, Todd S. "For Stern, It's Balk Radio: He Ends Bid For Governor." *The New York Times*, August 5, 1994.

"Radio Station Censors Itself After F.C.C. Action."
   *The New York Times*, April 25, 1987.

Ramirez, Anthony. "Howard Stern's Employer Vows
   To Appeal F.C.C. Fine." *The New York Times*,
   December 19, 1992.

———. "$1.7 Million To Settle Stern Radio Indecency
   Case." *The New York Times*, September 2, 1995.

Reilly, Patrick M.. "Disk Jockey Stern Is Making His
   Mark With His New Book 'Miss America.'" *The Wall
   Street Journal*, November 15, 1995.

Remnick, David. "The Accidental Anarchist." *The New
   Yorker*, March 10, 1997.

Roshan, Maer. "Poor Little Rich Boy." *New York*,
   November 20, 1995.

Sandler, Adam. "No Shock: 'Private Parts' Tops Disc
   Chart." *Variety*, March 6, 1997.

Sandomir, Richard. "In The Studio With Don Imus."
   *The New York Times*, September 29, 1993.

Stengel, Richard. "Radio Daze: The FCC tries to clear
   the air." *Time*, April 27, 1987.

Stuart, Reginald. "F.C.C. Acts To Restrict Indecent
   Programming." *The New York Times*, April 17, 1987.

Tomasky, Michael. "Fartman For Governor." *Voice*,
   April 5, 1994.

Weber, Bruce. "Now A Call From The G.W. Bridge:
   Stern To The Rescue." *The New York Times*,
   December 8, 1994.

"Which Dirty Words? When?" *The New York Times*,
   April 22, 1987.

Wilonsky, Robert. "Taking Howard Stern Seriously."
   *New Times*. February 27–March 5, 1997.

Zehme, Bill. "Keeping Up With The Sterns." *Esquire*,
   April 1997.

Zeidenberg, Leonard. "Indecency: Radio's Sound,
   FCC's Fury." *Broadcasting*, June 22, 1987.

### TELEVISION

*A&E Biography: Howard Stern Exposed: Howard Stern
   Radio Rebel*. ABC News Productions in association
   with A&E Network, 1996.

Joel, Ross. *Exposé: The History of Talk Radio*. Storyline
   Pictures, Inc., 1997.

## INDEX